To

Clara

for her patience and love

# Contents

# SKI TOURS
## in the
# SIERRA NEVADA

### Volume 3
### Yosemite
### Huntington and Shaver Lakes
### Kings Canyon
### Sequoia

## By Marcus Libkind

Bittersweet Publishing Company
Livermore, California

Cover design by Mac Smith.

Typography by Vera Allen Composition.

Front cover photograph by Kim Grandfield: Half Dome from Washburn Point.

Rear cover photograph by Lee Griffith.

All other photographs by author unless noted otherwise.

Acknowledgement: Over the years many people have been the source of invaluable information. They include National Forest Service, National Park Service and State Park personnel, the owners and operators of nordic centers and mountain shops, friends, and acquaintances. I am especially indebted to Brian Klimkowsky for his review of the manuscript and his thoughtful comments and ideas. Above all, I must thank Clara Yen for the many hours she spent editing the manuscript.

Library of Congress Catalog Card Number: 84-73452
International Standard Book Number: 0-931255-02-3

Published by Bittersweet Publishing Company
P.O. Box 1211, Livermore, California 94550

Printed in the United States of America

## KINGS CANYON

## SEQUOIA

## NORDIC SKI CENTERS

# Introduction

The guidebook series, *Ski Tours in the Sierra Nevada*, forms a comprehensive collection of ski tours which I have encountered during more than a decade of exploring the Sierra. They range geographically from the Lake Tahoe region in the north to Sequoia National Park in the south. The Lake Tahoe, Carson Pass, Bear Valley, Pinecrest, Yosemite, Huntington and Shaver Lakes, Kings Canyon and Sequoia areas are all covered in depth.

Whether you are a novice or an old timer, this series of guidebooks will introduce you to new and interesting areas which offer excellent ski touring opportunities. The information in these volumes will be useful for planning tours of an appropriate difficulty so you can enjoy more pleasurable and safer touring.

The 59 tours in this volume cover a large geographical area and are divided as follows:

> YOSEMITE—Tours originating in Yosemite National Park west of the Sierra Crest.

> HUNTINGTON AND SHAVER LAKES—Tours originating from or near Highway 168.

> KINGS CANYON—Tours originating in Kings Canyon National Park and Sequoia National Forest.

> SEQUOIA—Tours originating in Sequoia National Park.

I sincerely hope that the tours in these guidebooks will inspire you to explore new areas. I have thoroughly enjoyed the time spent in researching these books and I will be rewarded each time I meet another ski tourer who has found this information useful. As I would like to hear from you, let me know your comments and suggestions.

Marcus Libkind
P.O. Box 1211
Livermore, California 94550

# Author's Note

There are certain inherent dangers associated with wilderness travel in winter. No guidebook can diminish the hazards nor be a guarantee of safety. If you choose to experience the mountains in winter, you voluntarily do so knowing there are hazards.

Although the tour descriptions make reference to specific, obvious dangers, you should not assume that they are the only ones. Even the safest tour can become dangerous should you encounter poor weather, or adverse snow or avalanche conditions.

Some tours may take you through private property which is not marked. If you encounter marked private property, I hope that you will respect the property rights of others so that the good reputation of ski tourers will be preserved. Similarly, some tours pass through downhill ski resorts. For safety and to promote continued goodwill it is important to stay off the groomed slopes when ascending.

Although great care has gone into researching the tours in this guidebook, you may find inconsistencies due to factors such as new construction of roads and housing, policies toward plowing roads, changes in parking restrictions, and changes in trail markers. Also, extreme variations in snowfall can make a remarkable difference in how things appear. Be prepared to cope with these discrepancies should they arise.

In the final analysis, you must be responsible for executing your own safe trip.

Echo lake

End of Hwy 4

*Perfect backcountry touring*

# How To Use This Book

The short time it takes you to read this section will increase the usefulness of this guidebook. Each tour description in this guidebook contains a summary and a narrative. The summary box gives you at a glance the significant characteristics of the tour. The narrative is a description of the route.

Below is an explanation of each characteristic in the summary box.

**Difficulty:** The difficulty ratings are based on four criteria: length, elevation change, steepness, and navigation. A 5 level scale for rating the overall difficulty of the tours is used. The skills associated with each level are:

1—Beginner

- Little or no previous ski touring experience
- Follow simple directions without map or compass

2—Advancing beginner

- Proficiency in the basic techniques: diagonal stride, sidestep, kick turn, step turn, snowplow and snowplow turn
- Control speed on gradual downhills
- Negotiate short moderately steep terrain
- Follow simple directions in conjunction with a map

3—Intermediate

- Excellent proficiency in all the basic techniques plus the traverse and herringbone on moderately steep terrain
- Negotiate long moderately steep and short steep terrain
- Good stamina
- Navigate using a topographic map
- Use a compass to determine general orientation

4—Advancing intermediate

- Excellent proficiency in all ski touring techniques
- Negotiate long steep terrain including densely wooded areas
- Strong skier
- Navigate using a topographic map and compass

## 5—Expert

- Excellent all around ski tourer and mountain person
- Negotiate very steep terrain
- Exceptional endurance
- Navigate using a topographic map and compass

Two tours may be assigned the same rating but vary greatly in the skills required. For example, a tour on a road which is long and a tour which is short but requires navigation by map and compass may both be rated 3. For this reason the difficulty ratings should only be used as a general guide for selecting a tour of appropriate difficulty. Check the summary box for information regarding length, elevation and navigation to determine whether your abilities match the demands of a tour. Also, refer to the narrative which describes the tour route for special considerations.

The tours were rated assuming ideal snow conditions. Deep powder will make the traveling slower and more difficult. Ice, sometimes referred to as "Sierra cement," will make all tours much more difficult. If you are faced with icy conditions you might consider waiting until early afternoon to begin when hopefully the snow will have thawed.

**Length:** The length is an estimate of the horizontal mileage as obtained from the topographic maps. Several of the tours are in meadows which are adjacent to plowed roads and in these cases the length is simply stated as "short." Also noted is whether the distance is one-way or round trip.

**Elevation:** The first number is the elevation at the starting point of the tour in feet above sea level. The elevation is a major consideration when planning tours early or late in the season.

The elevation at the starting point is followed by a slash and the elevation change for the entire tour. The change is written as " + gain, – loss." "Nil" is used where the change is negligible.

**Navigation:** The navigational difficulty of each tour is based on untracked snow and good visibility. The key words and phrases are:

Adjacent to plowed road—Tour is located almost completely within sight of a plowed road.

Road—Tour follows snow-covered roads. Although roads are normally easy to follow, a small road or a road in open terrain may be difficult to locate or follow.

Marked trail—Tour follows marked trail; may require basic map-reading skills. Markers are normally brightly colored pieces of metal attached well above the snow level to trees or strips of brightly colored ribbon attached to tree branches close to the trail. Blazes which mark summer trails are not considered markers since they are often obscured by snow. In nearly all cases, when on a marked trail you must pay careful attention to locating each successive marker which may not be ideally placed. Even with a marked trail, you will probably need some knowledge of the route and basic map-reading skills to follow it.

Map—Tour requires the ability to read a topographic map since the tour follows well-defined terrain such as creeks, valleys, and ridges. Also remember that poor visibility can make route-finding impossible without a compass and expert knowledge of its use.

Compass—Tour requires the use of a compass in conjunction with a topographic map. In some instances the compass is mainly for safety but other routes require you to follow compass bearings.

*Hard work!*

**Time:** To give you a general idea of the length of time required to complete a tour, I have used the following key words and phrases:

- Short
- Few hours
- Half day
- Most of a day
- Full day
- Very long day
- One very long day or two days

Some of the factors which will affect your trip time include snow and weather conditions, your skiing ability and physical strength, characteristics of the tour, and your personal habits. Consideration has been given to reasonable rests and route finding in making the estimates.

Always keep in mind that the mid-winter months are filled with short days. Very long tours are best done in early spring when the days are longer.

**Season:** The season is the period in an average snowfall year during which the snow conditions for the tour are acceptable. Early and late in the season the conditions may be less than optimum. Exceptionally early or late snowfall as well as heavy snowfall, extend the season. On the other hand, during drought years the season may be shortened.

*Telemarks*                                    *Charlene Grandfield*

**USGS topo:** Listed are the United States Geological Survey topographic maps, both scale and name, which cover the tour route. Parts of these maps are reproduced in this guidebook, and the map reproduction number and its page location are at the beginning of each tour adjacent to the tour name. Be aware that some of these maps have been reduced.

For a majority of the tours only the 15' series maps are listed. The 7.5' series are also listed if they have significant benefit. When the elevations given for peaks are different on the two map series, the elevations stated in the text are from the map series reproduced in this book.

### Topographic Map Legend

| | |
|---|---|
| ● | Starting point |
| ▲ | Destination |
| 5 | Landmark number (corresponds to narrative) |
| ▬ | Highway or plowed road |
| ▬ ▬ | Ski route |

If you desire to purchase maps by mail you can obtain price and ordering information by contacting:

United States Geological Survey
Box 25286 Denver Federal Building
Denver, Colorado 80225

**Start and end:** Described are detailed directions for locating the starting and ending points of the tour. The ending point is omitted if the tour route returns to where it began.

Keep in mind that it may not be legal to park at these points. Increased usage and recent heavy snowfalls have resulted in greater restrictions and stricter enforcement. Sometimes carrying a snow shovel will allow you to clear a place to park. At other times you may have to resort to paying for parking or walking some distance. In the near future, the California "Sno-Park" bill should provide some relief from this situation.

The remainder of each tour description is in narrative form and describes the route. Keep in mind that the description is not a substitute for knowledge, skill and common sense. For your convenience, when a reference is made to the directions given in a different tour, the name of the tour is followed by the number, e.g. "Limit Trail Loop tour (no. 12)." Also, significant landmarks mentioned in the text are followed by a number in parentheses which corresponds to the same number found on the map, e.g. "From here descend to a road junction **(4)**."

*New snowfall*

# Yosemite

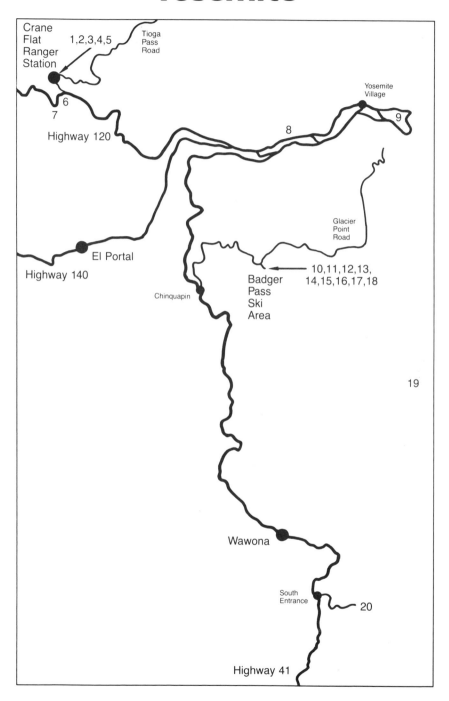

Crane Flat Ranger Station

1,2,3,4,5

Tioga Pass Road

Yosemite Village

6

7

9

8

Highway 120

Glacier Point Road

El Portal

10,11,12,13, 14,15,16,17,18

Highway 140

Chinquapin

Badger Pass Ski Area

19

Wawona

South Entrance

20

Highway 41

# 1 Crane Flat

MAP 1
PAGE 16

| | |
|---|---|
| Difficulty | 1 |
| Length | Short |
| Elevation | 6200/Nil |
| Navigation | Adjacent to plowed road |
| Time | Short |
| Season | December through early April |
| USGS topo | 15' series, Lake Eleanor |
| Start | Crane Flat Ranger Station (closed in winter). |

Crane Flat is the large meadow to the east of Crane Flat Ranger Station. This area is the best one in Yosemite for beginners to experience ski touring for the first time. Among the other tours in the Crane Flat area, the two particularly well-suited to novices are the Clark Range Vista and South Landing tours.

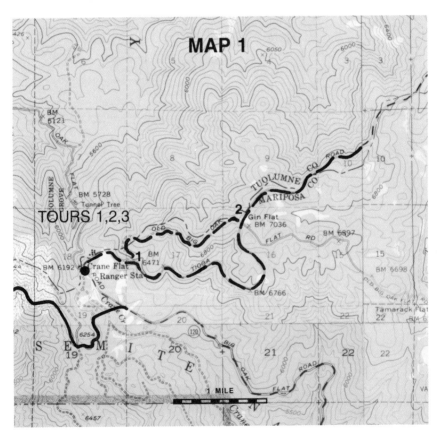

MAP **1**
PAGE 16

# Tioga Pass Road **2**

| | |
|---|---|
| Difficulty | 2–3 |
| Length | 6 miles round trip to Gin Flat or beyond |
| Elevation | 6200/ + 800, – 800 to Gin Flat |
| Navigation | Road |
| Time | Half day to full day |
| Season | December through early April |
| USGS topo | 15′ series, Lake Eleanor |
| Start | Crane Flat Ranger Station (closed in winter). |

This tour is on the easy to follow unplowed Tioga Pass Road. It is a gradual but continuous climb to Gin Flat, and beyond the road rolls for quite a distance. You can ski as far east as you desire; in theory you could even reach Tuolumne Meadows although it is not the shortest route and is a multi-day tour.

Leave the Crane Flat area by skiing east on snow-covered Tioga Pass Road. After you have skied 0.5 mile, you will pass Old Big Oak Flat Road **(1)** on your left. That road is marked and designated as trail number 4. It, too, goes to Gin Flat and may be combined with a tour on the Tioga Pass Road to make a loop tour.

Continue on Tioga Pass Road for another 2.7 miles to Gin Flat **(2)** which is the first level area you will find after leaving Crane Flat. When the snow is soft, the return run from Gin Flat is a pleasant downhill glide.

From Gin Flat, continue on the road for as far as you desire and then turn around.

# 3  Gin Flat Loop

MAP 1
PAGE 16

| | |
|---|---|
| Difficulty | 2 |
| Length | 6 miles round trip |
| Elevation | 6200/ + 800, − 800 |
| Navigation | Road |
| Time | Half day |
| Season | December through early April |
| USGS topo | 15′ series, Lake Eleanor |
| Start | Crane Flat Ranger Station (closed in winter). |

In this pleasant loop tour, you ski Old Big Oak Flat Road in one direction and Tioga Pass Road in the other. The two roads intersect at Gin Flat. The tour is a bit easier if you use Old Big Oak Flat Road for the ascent and Tioga Pass Road for the return trip.

From Crane Flat, ski east on Tioga Pass Road for 0.5 mile to the junction with Old Big Oak Flat Road (1). Old Big Oak Flat Road is marked and designated as trail number 4.

Turn north (left) onto Old Big Oak Flat Road and climb 700′ in 1.8 miles to its intersection with Tioga Pass Road at Gin Flat (2). According to legend, a keg of gin tumbled off a stagecoach here and miraculously did not break. Sheepherders found the keg, had a grand party, and named this place Gin Flat.

You complete the loop by skiing south (right) and then west on Tioga Pass Road back to Crane Flat.

*Tioga Pass Road*

# 4 Tuolumne Grove

MAP 2
PAGE 21

| | |
|---|---|
| Difficulty | 2 |
| Length | 3 miles round trip |
| Elevation | 6200/ + 500, − 500 |
| Navigation | Road |
| Time | Few hours |
| Season | January through mid-March |
| USGS topo | 15′ series, Lake Eleanor |
| Start | Crane Flat Ranger Station (closed in winter). |

It is a downhill run on Old Big Oak Flat Road to the Tuolumne Grove where the giant sequoias, largest of all living things, are an inspiring sight. You can make this tour during most of the winter months, but because the elevation drops well below 6000′, it is best to ski this tour during periods of heavy snowfall. The best time is at the tail end of a very cold storm while the snow is still relatively dry.

At the starting point, locate Old Big Oak Flat Road which is marked and designated as trail number 1. Descend to the north on this road for 1.3 miles to the turnaround point which is near the Tunnel Tree. The turnoff for the Tunnel Tree is on the east (right) side of Big Oak Flat Road and directly across from the first very large sequoia (8′ diameter) which you encounter on the west (left) side of the road.

If you enjoy downhill tours, you can continue skiing on Old Big Oak Flat Road. The 5.5 mile stretch from Crane Flat Ranger Station to Hodgdon Meadow and Big Oak Flat Entrance Station drops 1600′ and is nearly all downhill. Since the elevation at the end is below 5000′, you can only ski this route immediately after heavy snows and cold temperatures. Without these conditions, the tour will end with a hike. In any conditions, the snow will be wet at the lower elevations.

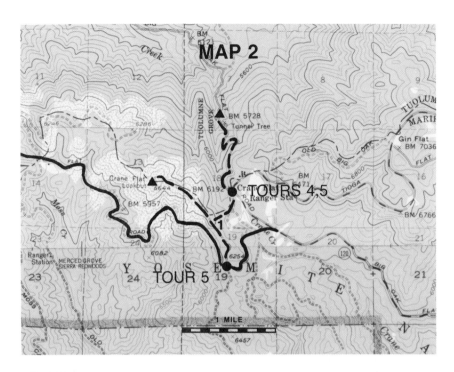

*Breaking trail*                              *Kim Grandfield*

# 5 Crane Flat Lookout

MAP 2
PAGE 21

| | |
|---|---|
| Difficulty | 2 |
| Length | 3 miles round trip |
| Elevation | 6200/ + 450, − 450 |
| Navigation | Road and marked trail |
| Time | Few hours |
| Season | December through early April |
| USGS topo | 15′ series, Lake Eleanor |
| Start | Highway 120, 0.7 mile west of the Crane Flat gas station or at the Crane Flat Ranger Station (both are closed in winter). |

During periods of high fire danger, Crane Flat Lookout is manned (or womanned). As you would expect, the lookout offers fine vistas in all directions.

If you choose to begin this tour on Highway 120, you should follow the road designated as trail number 6. This road leaves from the north side of the highway and ascends to Crane Flat Lookout.

On the other hand, if you choose to begin this tour at Crane Flat Ranger Station, you should first locate the road designated as trail number 5. Ski south on this road for 0.2 mile to the junction with trail number 7. Follow trail number 7 to the southwest (right) for 0.3 mile to its intersection with trail number 6 **(1)** which is the road to Crane Flat Lookout and begins on Highway 120. Turn northwest (right) and follow the road for 0.9 mile to the summit.

*Crane Flat*

# 6 Clark Range Vista

MAP 3
PAGE 25

| | |
|---|---|
| Difficulty | 2 |
| Length | 3 or 4 miles round trip |
| Elevation | 6150/ + 250, − 250 |
| Navigation | Road and marked trail |
| Time | Few hours |
| Season | December through early April |
| USGS topo | 15′ series, Lake Eleanor, El Portal |
| Start | Highway 120 at the turnoff to Crane Flat Campground. The turnoff is on the south side of the highway and 0.1 mile west of the Crane Flat gas station (closed in winter). If the campground road is plowed you can also start 0.4 mile down the road where trail number 10 begins. A third alternative is to start from the gas station. |

As you can guess from the title, this tour leads you to a point with views to the east of the Clark Range which looms above Yosemite Valley. This tour and the tour to South Landing offer the best touring in the Crane Flat area for beginners.

If you choose to begin the tour on the highway, ski or walk south on the campground road for 50 yards and locate the trail number 8 marker on the east (left) side of the road. Here, leave the campground road and carefully follow the number 8 markers to the southeast for 0.3 mile to the intersection with trail number 9 (1) which is adjacent to a meadow.

If you choose to begin the tour at the gas station, you must first locate the start of trail number 9 on the south side of Highway 120, 0.1 mile east of the gas station. Carefully follow the number 9 markers to the south for 0.3 mile to the intersection with trail number 8 (1) which is adjacent to a meadow.

At the junction of trails 8 and 9, enter the adjacent meadow and ski southeast (down the meadow) for a very short distance to a point where trail number 9 leaves the meadow to the south (right). Follow the number 9 markers for 100 yards to the next meadow and continue following them two-thirds of the way through the meadow. Here, look for the marked trail which enters the trees to the west (right). Continue on the trail for 0.2 mile to the intersection of trails 9 and 10 (2).

Trail number 9 intersects 10 on the Crane Flat Campground road. You can also reach this point from Highway 120 by driving south on the campground road for 0.4 mile. Occasionally, you may find the road unplowed, and you will have to ski the distance.

From the junction of trails 9 and 10, ski southeast for 1.4 miles on the snow-covered road, which is trail number 10, to Clark Range Vista. As you approach the vista, the road will become narrower as the vegetation seems to encroach on it; just continue on what appears to be the road.

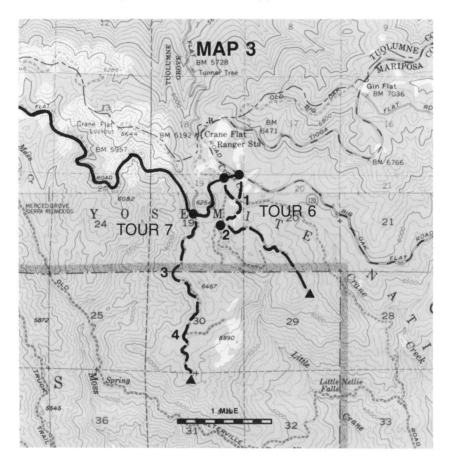

MAP 3
PAGE 25

# 7 South Landing

| | |
|---|---|
| Difficulty | 2 |
| Length | 5 miles round trip |
| Elevation | 6200/+200, −200 |
| Navigation | Road |
| Time | Half day |
| Season | December through early April |
| USGS topo | 15' series, El Portal |
| Start | Highway 120, 0.7 mile west of the Crane Flat gas station (closed in winter). |

The tour to South Landing is my favorite one in the Crane Flat area. The road gently rolls for the entire distance to South Landing and is perfect for beginners as well as advanced skiers who wish to get away from the more congested trails in the Crane Flat vicinity. To top it off, from South Landing the views of the Clark Range and the Merced River canyon are excellent; even better than those from Clark Range Vista.

From the south side of the highway, ski on the snow-covered road which weaves south. After 0.8 mile, you will reach a quarry and a fork in the road (**3**). The west (right) fork descends into the quarry; instead continue on the east (left) fork for 0.8 mile to a road junction (**4**).

At the junction, follow the road to the south (right) for 0.6 mile to its end at South Landing.

*Open slopes and spectacular vistas*

# Yosemite Valley 8

| | |
|---|---|
| Difficulty | 1–2 |
| Length | Up to 10 miles round trip |
| Elevation | 4000/Nil |
| Navigation | Adjacent to plowed road |
| Time | Short to full day |
| Season | Mid-winter whenever there is snow in Yosemite Valley. |
| USGS topo | 15′ series, Yosemite |
| Start | Anywhere in Yosemite Valley. |

If you happen to find yourself in Yosemite Valley when there is adequate snow-cover, or better yet, just after a storm, the valley is an ideal place to spend an entire day. It also offers sheltered areas when storm conditions prevent skiing at higher elevations.

Unfortunately, you cannot plan too far in advance for a ski touring trip in the valley because its very low elevation results in unpredictable snow conditions. But when there is snow, you can make tours to just about anywhere in the valley.

For a long tour, you can follow the Merced River from Happy Isles in the east to as far west as you desire. Ski in the meadows with their spectacular views of granite walls and waterfalls, or follow snow-covered paths through the trees. Also, you may want to consider skiing up Tenaya Creek as described in the Mirror Lake and Tenaya Canyon tour.

*Perfect meadow skiing* *Bob Bastasz*

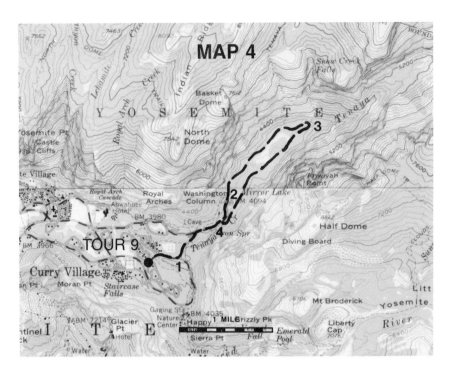

*Yosemite Valley*                                                    *Bob Bastasz*

MAP 4
PAGE 28

# Mirror Lake and Tenaya Canyon    9

| | |
|---|---|
| Difficulty | 1–2 |
| Length | Up to 5 miles round trip |
| Elevation | 4000/+100, −100 |
| Navigation | Road and trail (trail not marked but easy to follow) |
| Time | Few hours to half day |
| Season | Mid-winter whenever there is snow in Yosemite Valley. |
| USGS topo | 15′ series, Yosemite, Hetch Hetchy Reservoir |
| Start | Entrance to Pines Campgrounds. |

The tour to and beyond Mirror Lake follows Tenaya Creek from the east end of Yosemite Valley. During those special times when the valley floor is blanketed in white, this area becomes relatively secluded. The route offers views of the vertical walls and domes which form Tenaya Canyon.

You can use the free shuttle bus service in the valley to reach the starting point at Pines Campgrounds. From the entrance to the campgrounds, ski across the bridge over the Merced River and continue to ski east on the road for 0.3 mile to a road junction (**1**).

At the junction, turn north (left) and continue on the road for 0.2 mile to Tenaya Creek. Cross the creek and continue on the road for another 0.1 mile until you pass a road on your left. From here, travel another 0.5 mile to Mirror Lake (**2**).

From Mirror Lake, you continue northeast on a trail which parallels Tenaya Creek for 1.0 mile to a point where the Tenaya Lake and Tuolumne Meadows Trail leaves the canyon and zig-zags up the granite wall. You should continue on the trail which parallels Tenaya Creek for another 0.3 mile to a bridge (**3**) where you cross the creek.

Once on the other side of the creek, ski southwest on a trail for 1.2 miles back to Mirror Lake (**2**). Continue on the trail for another 0.2 mile to a bridge (**4**) where you again cross Tenaya Creek. You are now on the road you originally skied, and you can retrace it to the starting point.

# 10 Chinquapin Ski Trail

MAP 5
PAGE 31

| | |
|---|---|
| Difficulty | 3 |
| Length | 3 miles one-way |
| Elevation | 7200/ + 100, − 1300 |
| Navigation | Road and marked trail |
| Time | Short |
| Season | Late December through early April |
| USGS topo | 15′ series, Yosemite |
| Start | Badger Pass Ski Area on Glacier Point Road. |
| End | Chinquapin (intersection of Highway 41 and Glacier Point Road). |

This tour, with its 1300′ of continuous elevation loss, is lots of fun when the snow conditions are perfect; otherwise this tour is not much fun at all. Plan to do this tour during or immediately after a storm or on a warm day when the snow is of a soft, uniform consistency. Be aware that the entire descent is on a narrow road and requires an excellent ability to control speed. This road is part of what remains of Old Glacier Point Road.

At Badger Pass Ski Area, locate the Bruin chairlift and Bruin ski run. Climb up the run along the very north (right) edge of it. As you climb, look for an orange marker off to the side of the run which marks the start of trail number 7. The marker is located half of the distance up the Bruin chairlift. You should also be aware that about one-third of the distance up the chairlift is the ski area maintenance station, and at the station, you may find a Sno-Cat track on which you can ski to its intersection with trail number 7.

Follow the markers and road west as they traverse for 0.2 mile. Continue west on the road which parallels a creek drainage, which descends continuously, and which is at times steep. As you approach Chinquapin and the end of the tour, you will encounter the narrowest and steepest part of the tour. Be careful.

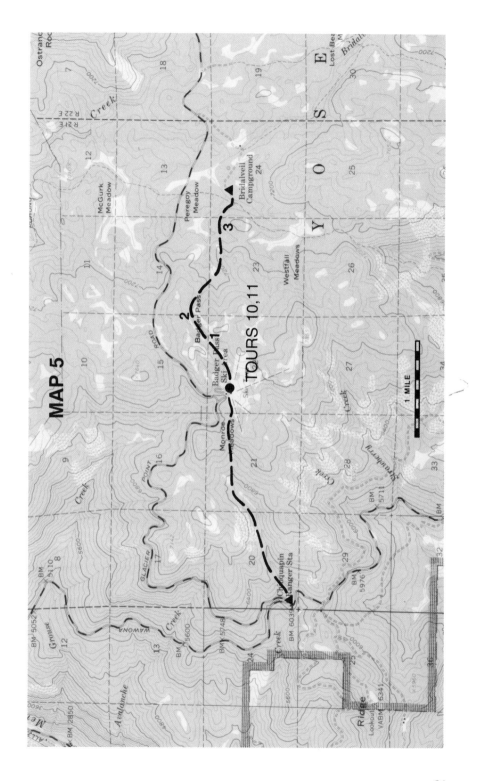

MAP 5

TOURS 10, 11

1 MILE

# **11** Old Glacier Point Road

MAP 5
PAGE 31

| | |
|---|---|
| Difficulty | 3 |
| Length | 5 miles round trip |
| Elevation | 7200/ + 800, − 800 |
| Navigation | Road and marked trail |
| Time | Half day |
| Season | December through mid-April |
| USGS topo | 15′ series, Yosemite |
| Start | Badger Pass Ski Area on Glacier Point Road. |

This tour follows one of the remaining sections of Old Glacier Point Road. This stretch, from the ski area at Badger Pass to Bridalveil Campground, is a pleasant tour through the trees. While this tour is worthy in its own right, you can use this tour to reach other destinations; for example: Summit Meadow which is on the route to Dewey Point; Limit Trail which leads to Westfall Meadows; and Peregoy Meadow which is one of the milestones on various other tours in the area.

At the east end of the ski area parking lot, locate the trail which heads northeast and parallels a Sno-Cat track and long narrow clearing. Follow this trail to the northeast for 0.5 mile to a level area (1).

As an alternative, you may start this tour at the side of the ski lodge which faces the chairlifts. Locate the Sno-Cat track which heads northeast up a narrow clearing and follow it for 0.5 mile to a level area (1). Here you must leave the Sno-Cat track and join the previously described trail. Look for a marker which identifies the point where you must leave the Sno-Cat track.

Continue on Old Glacier Point Road for 0.4 mile until you pass the cutoff to Summit Meadow on your left (2). Summit Meadow is located 0.4 mile to the north and over a small hill.

Again, continue on Old Glacier Point Road, pass a small meadow on your left, and travel to the Limit Trail junction (3) where there is another meadow to the north (left). There are signs marking this junction.

From the junction, continue east on Old Glacier Point Road for 0.6 mile to Bridalveil Campground. The campground is inaccessible by vehicle in the winter, and first-time snow campers sometimes choose it for their destination although camping in nearby Peregoy Meadow may be more pleasant.

Once in the campground, you can follow a road north for 0.5 mile to Glacier Point Road. If you continue straight on the road which you skied into the campground, you will intersect trail number 23 which leads to Westfall Meadows; if you follow the road even farther, you will intersect trail number 19 which is the Ghost Forest Trail.

*End of a hard trip*

# 12 Limit Trail Loop

MAP 6
PAGE 35

| | |
|---|---|
| Difficulty | 3 |
| Length | 7 miles round trip |
| Elevation | 7200/ + 1200, − 1200 |
| Navigation | Marked trail and map |
| Time | Most of a day |
| Season | December through mid-April |
| USGS topo | 15′ series, Yosemite |
| Start | Badger Pass Ski Area on Glacier Point Road. |

This loop covers sections of the Merced Crest Trail, Limit Trail, and Old Glacier Point Road. The terrain includes a series of gently sloping clearings and little-used meadows. You will find on this uncrowded route many outstanding vistas including views of Horse Ridge which borders Ostrander Lake and Buena Vista Peak.

Your first objective is to reach the top of Red Fox and Eagle chairlifts at Badger Pass Ski Area. From the lodge, ski northeast up a Sno-Cat track through a narrow clearing for 0.5 mile. Where the track levels (1), you will see a sign indicating that the Old Glacier Point Road trail leaves the track. Continue on the Sno-Cat track for 0.8 miles as it makes a loop around a small knob and leads to the top of the Beaver T-bar (2).

From the top of the T-bar, continue south on the Sno-Cat track for 0.5 mile as it climbs up a ridge to the top of Red Fox and Eagle chairlifts (3). You are now 600′ above the lodge and the view is a spectacular panorama.

At the top of the Red Fox chairlift, you will see a sign indicating that the Merced Crest Trail and Ostrander Lake are to the southeast. The route described here follows the Merced Crest Trail for 1.8 miles and is marked and designated as trail number 16.

From the top of the chairlift, ski down the gentle slope toward Peak 7855 which is known as Tempo Dome. Once at the base, traverse around the south side of the dome; at first you will climb slightly and then descend slightly. After you reach the southeast side of the dome, ski to the southeast down a steep hill for a short distance to the tree-filled saddle (4).

From the saddle, continue by following the markers, climbing gradually to the southeast until you reach the next landmark which is a broad, open highpoint (5). From the highpoint, ski down the clearing and then into the trees. Once in the trees, the route turns east, and you drop very sharply to a saddle (6). You are now at the junction of the Merced Crest Trail and Limit Trail. There is a sign on a tree indicating this spot.

From the trail junction, ski north on the Limit Trail which is marked and designated as trail number 13. In 0.2 mile, you will enter Westfall Meadows. Except for a short distance when the marked trail leaves and returns to the meadow on its west (left) side, you travel north through 0.7 mile long Westfall Meadows.

From the meadows' most northern point, gradually descend north for 0.5 mile, passing between two high points, until you reach the next meadow **(7)**. At this meadow, you have several choices.

Just as you reach the meadow, signs will indicate two of the alternatives. To the east (right), the Old Glacier Point Road trail leads to Bridalveil Campground. Don't make this turn. Another sign points north (straight). If you follow this northern route, you will intersect Glacier Point Road in 0.5 mile. You will then have to ski another 1.3 miles west on the road to Summit Meadow and another 1.1 miles to Badger Pass. You can find details for this route in the Westfall Meadows tour.

This tour, however, continues west (left) on the Old Glacier Point Road trail; markers will be visible intermittently. Ski west for 1.0 mile to the junction of the Summit Meadow cutoff **(8)**. From the cutoff, continue southwest for 0.5 mile on the Old Glacier Point Road trail until it levels. Just ahead, you will reach the top of a long and narrow clearing. From the top of the clearing, either continue southwest on the trail which parallels the clearing on its north (right) side, or ski down the clearing itself. Either way, you will reach the lodge at Badger Pass Ski Area in 0.5 mile.

You can also ski this tour in the reverse direction in order to take advantage of a downhill run at the ski area. If you do so, you will find the Beaver and Rabbit runs the least difficult. This tour skied in the reverse direction is shorter by 1.0 mile.

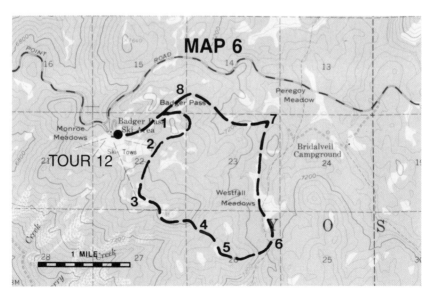

*Half Dome*                                    *Kim Grandfield*

MAP 7
PAGE 39

# Glacier Point Road 13

| | |
|---|---|
| Difficulty | 1–4 |
| Length | Up to 22 miles round trip |
| Elevation | 7200/Up to +2000, −2000 |
| Navigation | Road |
| Time | Up to very long day |
| Season | December through mid-April |
| USGS topo | 15′ series, Yosemite |
| Start | Badger Pass Ski Area on Glacier Point Road. |

If you travel the entire distance to Glacier Point, you will be treated to spectacular views of Yosemite Valley 3200′ below, Half Dome, Vernal and Nevada Falls, plus vistas of the impressive Clark Range to the east. Best of all, you will have the opportunity to enjoy this beauty in peace since most tourists are stopped by the snow-covered road.

There are several other landmarks along Glacier Point Road which you can choose as a destination. The most significant ones are Summit Meadow at 1.1 miles and Peregoy Meadow at 2.8 miles. Glacier Point Road is also the access route to several other tours in the area.

Only in the last several years has the entire distance from Badger Pass Ski Area to Glacier Point on Glacier Point Road been groomed. With the groomed track, you may find it more feasible to make the round trip to Glacier Point in one day. Still, this very long tour requires considerable stamina. Many people choose to make this tour into an overnighter by snow camping at Glacier Point. If you do an overnight trip, obtain a permit at the Badger Pass Ski Area ranger station.

Locate the Glacier Point Road Trailhead at the north end of the Badger Pass Ski Area parking lot. Ski north on this trail for 0.1 mile to the intersection with snow-covered Glacier Point Road.

Ski northeast (right) on Glacier Point Road for 1.0 mile until you reach Summit Meadow (2) on the south (right) side of the road. The short distance and minimal elevation change make the tour to Summit Meadow an excellent choice for beginners. Once there, you can spend time practicing both in the flat area and on the adjacent slopes.

Two routes from the Summit Meadow area to Dewey Point are described separately in this guidebook. If you are a beginner who has conquered Summit Meadow and want to go farther, you are encouraged to ski the first 0.7 mile of the Dewey Point Meadow Trail (no. 14).

The tour to Glacier Point continues east on the snow-covered road. In the next 1.3 miles, you will drop 250′ until you pass the trail to Westfall Meadows on your right. Continue for another 0.4 mile on Glacier Point Road to Peregoy Meadow (3). There will be a sign that indicates the

# 13

Bridalveil Trailhead.

To reach Glacier Point, you continue on Glacier Point Road for 0.5 mile until you reach Bridalveil Creek. Continuing for another 0.9 mile brings you to Bridalveil Creek Trail **(4)** which leads to Ostrander Lake; another 0.7 mile brings you to Horizon Ridge Trail **(5)** which also leads to Ostrander Lake.

To reach Glacier Point, continue on the road for 0.3 mile until it turns north. Continue north on the road, as it climbs 600′ in the next 4.0 miles and passes Pothole Meadows, until you reach a point adjacent to Sentinel Dome **(6)**. If time permits, you can ascend Sentinel Dome as a side trip. The top of the dome, crowned with a famous gnarled Jeffrey pine, is 0.5 mile off the main road.

Finally, from the point adjacent to Sentinel Dome **(6)**, descend 1.6 miles and 600′ to Glacier Point. This last section is the most difficult one of the entire tour.

*Glacier Point Road*                                          *Bob Bastasz*

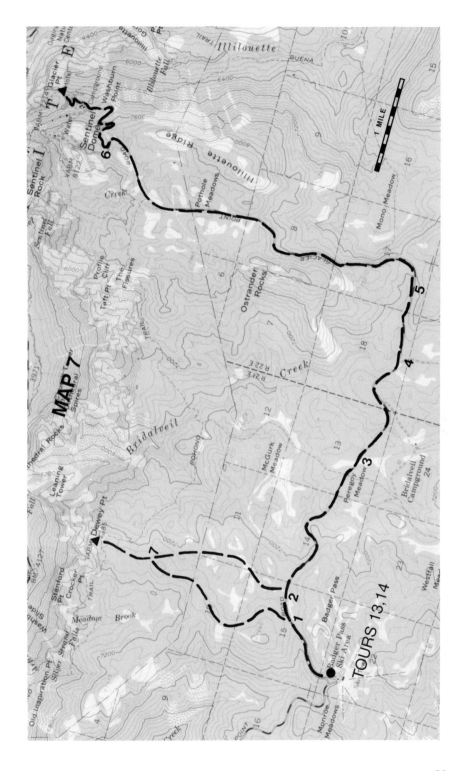

TOURS 13,14

MAP 7

1 MILE

39

# 14 Dewey Point

MAP 7
PAGE 39

| | |
|---|---|
| Difficulty | 3 |
| Length | 7 miles round trip |
| Elevation | 7200/ + 700, − 700 |
| Navigation | Road and marked trail |
| Time | Most of a day |
| Season | December through mid-April |
| USGS topo | 15′ series, Yosemite |
| Start | Badger Pass Ski Area on Glacier Point Road. |

The classic tour in the Yosemite area is the tour to Dewey Point. To avoid the weekend crowds, visit this area mid-week. No matter how crowded, this tour is worth the effort and should not be missed by anyone. The reward for reaching Dewey Point is a spectacular view of Yosemite Valley below.

From the Badger Pass Ski Area, follow the Glacier Point Road tour (no. 13) for 0.8 mile to a crest (**1**) where it starts to descend very gradually to Summit Meadow. At the crest on the north (left) side of the road, a sign marks the beginning of the Ridge Trail to Dewey Point. If you continue on Glacier Point Road for an additional 0.3 mile to Summit Meadow (**2**), you will find a sign on the north (left) side of the road marking the easier and more popular Meadow Trail which also leads to Dewey Point.

**Meadow Trail.** The Meadow Trail to Dewey Point is marked and designated as trail number 18. From Glacier Point Road (**2**), ski north on the Meadow Trail for 0.2 mile until you enter a meadow. Ski north along the east (right) side of the meadow for 0.5 mile to its north end.

At the north end of the meadow, enter the trees and ski north for about 0.2 mile to the top of a small hill. You will find this hill perfect for practicing turns as I did when I was learning to cross-country ski.

From the top of this hill, continue north on the Meadow Trail for about 0.7 mile to an intersection with the Ridge Trail (**7**). Continue north along the Meadow and Ridge Trails, which have merged, for another 0.6 mile to Dewey Point. These last 1.3 miles are filled with small but challenging ups and downs.

Once you have reached the rim overlooking Yosemite Valley, you can ski in either direction along the rim to get away from the crowds.

**Ridge Trail.** The Ridge Trail to Dewey Point is marked and designated as trail number 14. Ski north from Glacier Point Road (**1**) and follow the trail for 0.7 mile as it traverses around a highpoint and leads to the top of a ridge.

Once on the ridge, you continue north along it for 1.2 miles to the intersection of the Ridge Trail and the Meadow Trail (**7**). Along the ridge, there are some open spots which offer fine views, and the skiing here is very pleasant.

From the intersection of the Ridge and Meadow Trails, you now follow the two of them to Dewey Point which is located 0.6 mile to the north.

*Meadow Trail to Dewey Point*                                    *Bob Bastasz*

# 15 Westfall Meadows

MAP 8
PAGE 43

| | |
|---|---|
| Difficulty | 3 |
| Length | 7 miles round trip |
| Elevation | 7200/ + 600, − 600 |
| Navigation | Road and marked trail |
| Time | Most of a day |
| Season | December through mid-April |
| USGS topo | 15' series, Yosemite |
| Start | Badger Pass Ski Area on Glacier Point Road. |

The tour to Westfall Meadows is an excellent choice for advancing beginner skiers who have mastered the basic techniques and desire a little adventure. Plan to eat lunch at Westfall Meadows and enjoy the solitude.

From the Glacier Point Road Trailhead which is located at the north end of the Badger Pass Ski Area parking lot, ski north for 0.1 mile to the intersection with Glacier Point Road. Turn northeast (right) and follow the road for 1.0 mile to Summit Meadow (**1**).

From Summit Meadow, continue on Glacier Point Road for 1.3 miles as it quickly drops 250' until you reach the turnoff to Westfall Meadows (**2**). The turnoff is on the south (right) side of the road, and a sign will be located there. Note that if you reach Peregoy Meadow, you have passed the turnoff by 0.5 mile.

At the turnoff, turn south onto the marked trail which you now follow to Westfall Meadows. After leaving Glacier Point Road, you ski through trees, then through a meadow, then into the trees again, and finally into another meadow. At the south end of the second meadow, find the junction with Old Glacier Point Road (**3**). You are now 0.5 mile from Glacier Point Road.

South of Old Glacier Point Road, the trail to Westfall Meadows is called the Limit Trail and is designated as trail number 13. Continue south on this trail for 0.5 mile to the northern edge of Westfall Meadows. The meadows are 0.7 mile long.

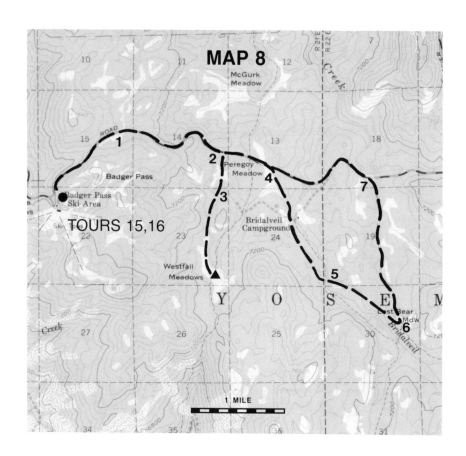

43

# 16 Ghost Forest Loop

MAP 8
PAGE 43

|  |  |
|---|---|
| Difficulty | 3 |
| Length | 11 miles round trip |
| Elevation | 7200/ + 650, − 650 |
| Navigation | Road and marked trail |
| Time | Full day |
| Season | Late December through early April |
| USGS topo | 15′ series, Yosemite |
| Start | Badger Pass Ski Area on Glacier Point Road. |

Once you leave Glacier Point Road, the Ghost Forest Loop tour is a pleasant tour through the woods. The route is quite level and offers a little adventure for skiers only accustomed to skiing on roads. Tourers who have been to Ostrander Lake by one of the standard routes might consider skiing the Ghost Forest Trail which intersects the Bridalveil Trail at Lost Bear Meadow.

Begin this tour by following the Glacier Point Road tour (no. 13) for 2.8 miles to Peregoy Meadow (**4**). You will find a sign at Peregoy Meadow indicating the Bridalveil Trailhead.

Near the trailhead sign, locate the marked Ghost Forest Trail, designated as trail number 19, where it intersects Glacier Point Road. Follow the trail south along the east edge of the meadow for 0.4 mile to the southern end of the meadow. At the southern end, cross the west fork of Bridalveil Creek to its west side.

Once you are on the west side of the creek, ski south and parallel to the creek. At a point 0.9 mile from the southern end of Peregoy Meadow, you cross back to the east side of the west fork of Bridalveil Creek (**5**). In mid-winter, the creek is covered with snow and this crossing is trivial. Early or late in the ski season, some care may be required. If necessary, look for a nearby log on which to cross.

Once you have crossed the creek, ski southeast and parallel to the creek for 1.0 mile to Lost Bear Meadow (**6**) which is now wooded. Here you intersect Bridalveil Creek Trail, one of the standard routes to Ostrander Lake which lies to the southeast.

From Lost Bear Meadow, follow Bridalveil Creek Trail north (left) for 1.2 miles to the east fork of Bridalveil Creek where you cross it. From the creek, continue for 0.3 mile to the intersection with Glacier Point Road (**7**). Once you are at the road, ski west (left) on it for 1.2 miles to Peregoy Meadow (**4**). Continue west on the road for another 2.8 miles to Badger Pass Ski Area.

44

*Bridalveil Trail*

*Ostrander Lake Hut*

MAP 9
PAGE 49

# Ostrander Lake **17**

| | |
|---|---|
| Difficulty | 4 |
| Length | 9 miles one-way |
| Elevation | 7200/+1950, −600 one-way via Bridalveil Creek Trail or 7200/+2100, −750 via Horizon Ridge Trail |
| Navigation | Road, marked trail and map |
| Time | Two days round trip |
| Season | Mid-December through mid-April |
| USGS topo | 15' series, Yosemite |
| Start | Badger Pass Ski Area on Glacier Point Road. |
| End | Ostrander Lake Hut. |

During the winter months, the ranger station at Ostrander Lake is converted into a ski hut. For ski tourers desiring a multi-day trip, the hut is a popular destination. The tour combines winding through woods and traversing along ridges with many spectacular views. The hut is located on the edge of Ostrander Lake where corniced Horse Ridge rises from the opposite shore.

There are accommodations for 23 at the hut and a reservation system has been instituted to insure sufficient space for those planning to stay overnight. For reservations, obtain an application from:

Yosemite Natural History Association
P.O. Box 545
Yosemite National Park, California 95389

Make your plans early because it is necessary to submit an application during the first two weeks of October. The natural history association who employs a winter caretaker charges a fee for use of the hut.

There are three distinct routes to Ostrander Lake. Of the two primary trails, Bridalveil Creek Trail and Horizon Ridge Trail, Bridalveil Creek Trail is easier. These routes will be described here. The third route, Merced Crest Trail, is significantly more difficult and is described separately.

You can combine Bridalveil Creek Trail and Horizon Ridge Trail to form a pleasant loop trip to and from Ostrander Lake and enjoy considerable variation in terrain. If you use Horizon Ridge for the return trip, the ridge offers an outstanding downhill run when the conditions are right. Most people take a full day to ski to or return from the hut. Adding a layover day at the hut makes the tour more leisurely and gives you the opportunity to explore beautifully corniced Horse Ridge which dominates the view from the hut.

**Bridalveil Creek Trail.** Begin this tour by following the Glacier Point Road tour (no. 13) for 2.8 miles to Peregoy Meadow (**1**). Here you will

# 17

find a sign indicating the Bridalveil Trailhead and the start of the Ghost Forest Loop trail.

The Ghost Forest Loop tour (no. 16) intersects Bridalveil Creek Trail at Lost Bear Meadow (3), and you can use it as an alternative route. This alternative slightly shortens the tour, but the conditions tend to be poor early and late in the season.

To follow the standard route, continue east on Glacier Point Road for 1.2 miles to the junction with Bridalveil Creek Trail (2) which is marked with a sign. Bridalveil Creek Trail is well marked, and even during a heavy snowfall the route can be found with considerable care.

Ski south from Glacier Point Road along the Bridalveil Creek Trail for 0.3 mile and cross the east fork of Bridalveil Creek. Continue for another 1.2 miles to Lost Bear Meadow (3). Lost Bear Meadow, which is now wooded, is located near the west fork of Bridalveil Creek.

From Lost Bear Meadow, you continue by skiing southeast along the marked trail which parallels the west fork of Bridalveil Creek. After you have skied about a mile from Lost Bear Meadow, follow the trail as it heads away from the creek and then begins to climb. At the point where it begins to climb (4), you have covered almost 75 percent of the mileage to Ostrander Lake, but nearly all the elevation gain remains.

Bridalveil Creek Trail now heads east, and you continue by climbing along it. Cross a large clearing and then continue for 1.0 mile to the junction of Bridalveil Creek Trail and Horizon Ridge Trail (5).

About 50 yards past the trail junction, you reach a large clearing which climbs to the southeast. This hill is aptly called Heart Attack Hill, and you climb to its top (6). There is a grand view to the east and north from this point. With the High Sierra as a backdrop, Mt. Starr King, Mt. Clark, and the Clark Range lie before you.

Locate the spot a short distance before the top of the hill where the winter trail leaves the summer trail. Follow the marked winter trail which heads south as it climbs gradually around to the south side of Peak 8641 and then drops down to Ostrander Lake and the ski hut.

**Horizon Ridge Trail.** To reach the start of Horizon Ridge Trail, follow Glacier Point Road to Bridalveil Creek Trail (2) which is located 4.0 miles from the starting point. Continue east on Glacier Point Road for 0.7 mile to Horizon Ridge Trail (7). This junction point will be marked with a sign, and the trail will be marked and designated as number 15.

Follow Horizon Ridge Trail for 1.6 miles to the southeast over rolling terrain and through woods to the base of Horizon Ridge (8). Climb up the open ridge which offers many vistas. Continue southeast and pass the highest point of the ridge, Peak 8262, to its west.

After you pass Peak 8262, you descend to the southeast for 0.5 mile to

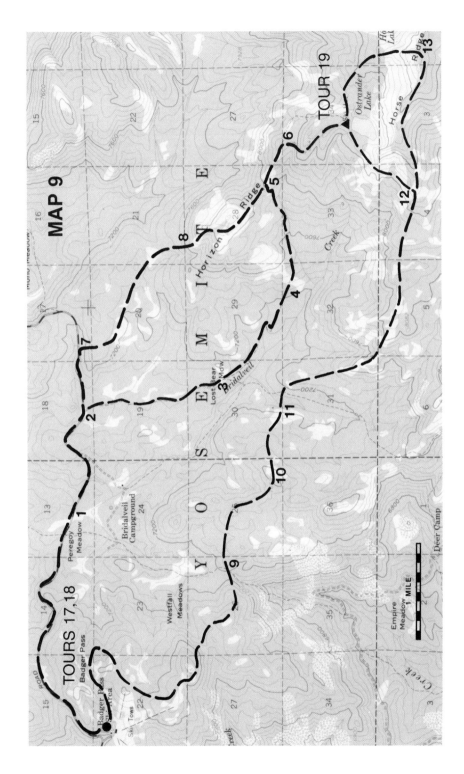

MAP 9

TOURS 17,18

TOUR 19

49

# 17

the intersection with Bridalveil Creek Trail at the base of Heart Attack Hill (**5**). From the base, follow the route as described for Bridalveil Creek Trail to Ostrander Lake.

*Rime encrusted tree*

MAP **9**
PAGE 49

# Merced Crest Trail **18**

| | |
|---|---|
| Difficulty | 4 |
| Length | 10 miles one-way |
| Elevation | 7200/ + 2750, − 1400 |
| Navigation | Marked trail and map |
| Time | Full day one-way |
| Season | Mid-December through mid-April |
| USGS topo | 15′ series, Yosemite |
| Start | Badger Pass Ski Area on Glacier Point Road. |
| End | Ostrander Lake Hut. |

Ostrander Lake in Yosemite's backcountry is situated in a bowl formed by Horse Ridge. Two routes to the lake and the neighboring ski hut are described in the previous tour. The Merced Crest Trail is a third alternative for reaching this destination. Of the three routes, this one is by far the most demanding.

There are good reasons for choosing the Merced Crest Trail. For some, the difficulty is an irresistible challenge, and for everyone, there is incomparable solitude. Along this route, the trail traverses ridges with spectacular vistas and crosses three drainages which require care in descent and effort to ascend.

The Merced Crest Trail can be combined with either of the other two routes to Ostrander Lake to form a loop. Even though the route described here is from Badger Pass Ski Area to the lake, this route is more commonly skied from the lake to the ski area in order to minimize the uphill climbing. This route is also more difficult to follow than the other two and is more exposed to the wind. It is best to ski this route in warm, fair weather when ice and route-finding are not problems.

The first 3.6 miles of this tour are identical to the Limit Trail Loop tour (no. 12). Refer to that tour description for directions to the junction of the Merced Crest Trail and Limit Trail (**9**). These first miles are representative of the varying terrain which follows.

At the saddle and sign which denotes the junction of the Merced Crest Trail and Limit Trail (**9**), the Merced Crest Trail continues southeast and continues to be marked and designated as trail number 16.

Ski to the southeast for 1.2 miles and climb 450′ to the top of Peak 7652 (**10**). Then, descend to the east for 0.8 mile and drop 550′ to the intersection with one of the tributaries of the west fork of Bridalveil Creek (**11**). At the bottom of this third and final large drop, you have skied 5.6 miles and are 100′ lower than the elevation at the start of the tour. You will find the next leg of the tour is a 3.0 mile continuous climb toward Horse Ridge.

# 18

Cross Bridalveil Creek and ski east for 0.2 mile to the base of a ridge. Ski up this ridge to the south for 1.3 miles and 800′ until the route levels. You then continue for 1.4 miles along a broad ridge which leads to Horse Ridge. Along this broad ridge, the trail stays on the north side of the crest.

As you ski along the ridge, you should look for a bowl to the north. Drop into the bowl **(12)**, following the markers if possible, and traverse to the northeast. At the north end of the bowl, veer slightly east, and you will soon reach Ostrander Lake. The ski hut is located on the north side of the lake. Refer to the Ostrander Lake tour for details on reservations at the hut.

*Lunch stop on Horizon Ridge Trail*

MAP **9**
PAGE 49

# Horse Ridge Loop **19**

| | |
|---|---|
| Difficulty | 3 |
| Length | 4 miles round trip |
| Elevation | 8600/ + 800, − 800 |
| Navigation | Map |
| Time | Half day |
| Season | Mid-December through mid-April |
| USGS topo | 15′ series, Yosemite |
| Start | Ostrander Lake Hut. See below for more details. |

Spectacular Horse Ridge rises abruptly from Ostrander Lake and dominates the view. Since the Horse Ridge Loop tour begins at Ostrander Lake Hut, plan to do this tour on your layover day at the hut. The Ostrander Lake and Merced Crest Trail tours give details about the alternative routes for reaching the lake and the ski hut located at its edge.

From the ski hut at Ostrander Lake, ski east and follow the Hart Lakes Trail for 0.6 mile until you reach a spur to the south which rises to the top of Horse Ridge. Follow it, first climbing gradually, then climbing at a steep angle, to the top of Horse Ridge **(13)**. The last 150′ are very steep.

The broad summit of Horse Ridge is dotted with trees. Fog and winds from the south often cause ice, known as rime, to form in the trees. The wind also causes the formation of cornices on the north side of the ridge.

Ski to the west and gradually downhill along Horse Ridge. While enjoying the solitude and beauty of the setting, be sure to stay away from the north edge.

After you have skied 1.5 miles along the ridge **(12)**, find a safe route and descend to the northeast into a bowl. The Merced Crest Trail, which is marked and designated as trail number 16, passes through this bowl and leads to Ostrander Lake. Traverse the bowl to the northeast and at the north end veer slightly east. You will soon reach Ostrander Lake.

A few words of caution: if there is avalanche danger, do not attempt this tour. Talk to the hut caretaker if you are unsure.

# 20 Mariposa Grove

MAP 10
PAGE 55

| | |
|---|---|
| Difficulty | 2–3 |
| Length | Up to 7 miles round trip |
| Elevation | 5600/Up to +1200, −1200 |
| Navigation | Road |
| Time | Up to most of a day |
| Season | Late December through March |
| USGS topo | 15' series, Yosemite |
| Start | Mariposa Grove where the road is no longer plowed. From the south entrance of the park on Highway 41 drive east to the Mariposa Grove. |

The Mariposa Grove is an excellent place to ski among the giant sequoias, the largest of living things. This tour which is entirely on roads, passes through both the Lower and Upper Groves where many famous trees are located. This tour also takes you to Wawona Point which gives you a view of the Wawona area almost 3000' below. Enjoy this outstanding area in the quiet of a winter afternoon.

From the parking area, ski to the east and north on the snow-covered road. As you climb steadily, you first pass through the Lower Grove. Look for the Grizzly Giant, the largest of the trees in the Mariposa Grove and the fifth-largest known sequoia, located 0.7 mile from the start of the tour and a short distance off the road to the north and west (left).

From the Grizzly Giant, continue skiing on the road for 1.6 miles to a junction (1). The two roads ahead of you connect to make a 1.5 mile loop through the Upper Grove. If you ski the loop in a clockwise direction, the downhill section is less steep.

From the junction, follow the road to the east (left) for 0.5 mile to a saddle and another junction (2). This junction is the location of the turn-off to Wawona Point.

To reach Wawona Point from the junction, ski on the road for 0.5 mile which leads northwest (left) up a ridge. Wawona Point is a fine place to enjoy lunch.

From the junction (2), continue south (right) for 0.1 mile until you reach the Fallen Wawona Tunnel Tree. From here you ski down the road for 0.4 mile until you pass the Telescope Tree on your left, and continue for another 0.4 mile to an interpretive museum which is open in winter. Ski 0.1 mile farther on the road and you will reach the loop starting point (1).

One final note: During and immediately after a large storm, the road from the entrance station which is normally plowed east for 2.0 miles may not be passable. In this case the tour will be 2.0 miles longer in each direction and you will have an additional 500' of elevation gain.

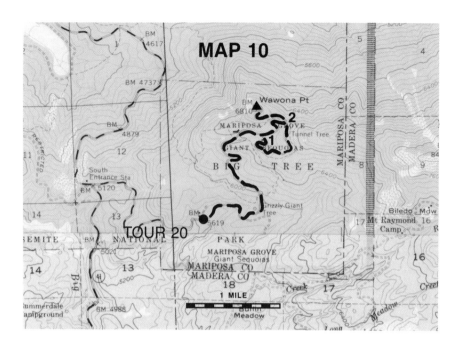

*Spring skiing*

*Easy touring*                                    *Kim Grandfield*

# Huntington and Shaver Lakes

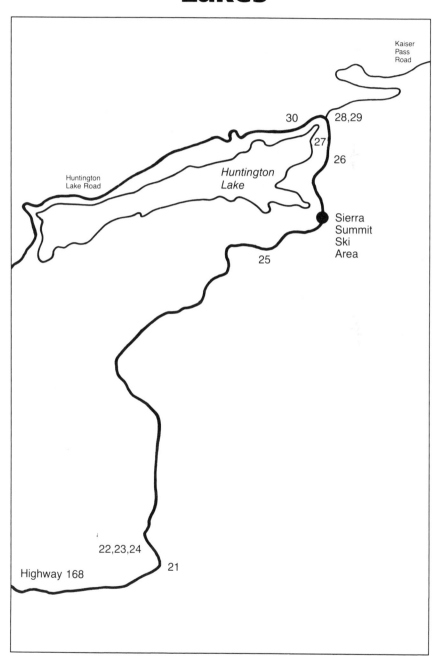

Kaiser Pass Road

30    28,29
      27
      26

Huntington
Lake Road

*Huntington
Lake*

Sierra
Summit
Ski
Area

25

22,23,24    21

Highway 168

MAP 11
PAGE 59

# 21 Tamarack Ridge

| | |
|---|---|
| Difficulty | 1–3 |
| Length | Up to more than 10 miles |
| Elevation | 7550/Elevation change depends on route chosen |
| Navigation | Road and marked trail |
| Time | Up to full day |
| Season | December through April |
| USGS topo | 15' series, Huntington Lake; 7.5' series, Huntington Lake |
| Start | Tamarack Ridge Trailhead on Highway 168, 6.8 miles east of the Big Creek turnoff. |

Many different trails which are dedicated to ski touring, to snowmobiling, and to dual use begin at Tamarack Ridge Trailhead. Even though this area is heavily used, these trails offer some of the best beginner ski touring in the Huntington and Shaver Lakes area.

Due to the great number of trails in this area, descriptions of each one will not be included. Instead, a brief description of the groups of trails will be given. If you are interested in skiing in this area, it will be useful to obtain a 7.5' series Huntington Lake topo.

At the starting point, locate the main trail which heads southeast. Ski along this trail for 0.2 mile to a major trail junction (1). If the snow conditions are very poor in this short section, do not be discouraged; they will improve.

At the junction, you must make a decision as to which area you want to explore. To the left are the Chipmunk, Porcupine and Raccoon trails. There are a total of about 4 miles of trail in this area which make up three small loops.

To the right from the junction is the Raven trail. There are also about 4 miles of trail here.

Straight ahead from the junction is a fork in the road. The left fork is a snowmobile trail and the right fork is a dual use trail which connects with the Raven trail. This right fork can be followed to Cutts Meadow as shown on the map.

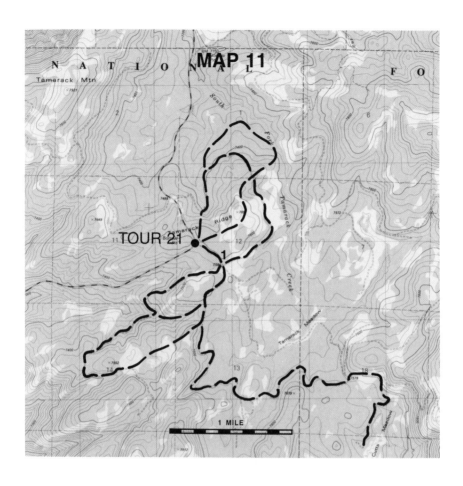

MAP 11

TOUR 21

1 MILE

*Snow cave*

MAP 12
PAGE 63

# Eagle Trail to Shaver Lake Vista

# 22

| | |
|---|---|
| Difficulty | 2 |
| Length | 4 miles round trip |
| Elevation | 7450/ + 300, − 300 |
| Navigation | Road |
| Time | Half day |
| Season | December through April |
| USGS topo | 15′ series, Huntington Lake; 7.5′ series, Huntington Lake |
| Start | Coyote Nordic Trailhead, 0.4 mile north of Tamarack Ridge Trailhead. |

Coyote Nordic Trailhead is the beginning of several excellent tours into an area where snowmobiles are excluded. The tour to Shaver Lake Vista is the easiest one in the area, yet it offers the finest views. A leisurely lunch at the vista is an excellent way to enjoy the panoramic view of Shaver Lake and the foothills below.

From the trailhead, ski southwest for 0.2 mile to a trail junction (1). At the junction, take the south (left) fork and start to climb gradually uphill for another 0.7 mile until you pass the Marmot Trail turnoff on your right (2).

Continue on the road for 0.7 mile farther and pass a road, the Grizzly Trail turnoff, on your right (3). Just ahead you will reach a high point.

Continue on the road which will drop, climb, and then become level. About 0.2 mile after it levels, you must turn west (left) off the road to reach Shaver Lake Vista. Look for the sign which marks the turnoff point.

If you are an intermediate skier, you may want to consider the Coyote Trail Loop tour which takes you to Huntington Lake Vista as well as Shaver Lake Vista.

# 23 Coyote Trail Loop

MAP 12
PAGE 63

| | |
|---|---|
| Difficulty | 3 |
| Length | 5 miles round trip |
| Elevation | 7450/ + 500, − 500 |
| Navigation | Road and marked trail |
| Time | Half day |
| Season | December through April |
| USGS topo | 15′ series, Huntington Lake; 7.5′ series, Huntington Lake |
| Start | Coyote Nordic Trailhead, 0.4 mile north of Tamarack Ridge Trailhead. |

Of all the tours which originate at Coyote Nordic Trailhead, this loop tour is the best. The tour takes you to two spectacular vista points, Huntington Lake Vista and Shaver Lake Vista.

From the trailhead, ski 0.2 mile southwest to a trail junction (1). The two forks connect to form Coyote Trail Loop. The route described here heads in a counterclockwise direction and is slightly easier than the clockwise direction.

At the trail junction, take the north (right) fork and ski on it for 0.5 mile until you pass the Marmot Trail turnoff on your left. About 50 yards ahead on your right is the Grizzly Trail turnoff (4).

Continue straight ahead on Coyote Trail for 0.6 mile to an intersection with a road which cuts across the trail (5). This road is part of Grizzly Trail.

Again continue straight ahead on Coyote Trail as it climbs for 0.4 mile to the ridge top of which Tamarack Mountain is a part. Once on the ridge, you follow the trail which turns southwest and traverses along the west side of the ridge for 0.4 mile to Huntington Lake Vista (6) which is marked by a sign.

From Huntington Lake Vista, continue southwest on the marked trail. You can expect to drop 200′ before the trail levels out and approaches Shaver Lake Vista (7). To reach Shaver Lake Vista, which is 0.7 mile from Huntington Lake Vista, look for the sign marking the turnoff and ski a short distance to the west (right) off the trail.

From Shaver Lake Vista, the route to the trailhead is also known as Eagle Trail. From the vista point, return to the main trail. Next, ski east for 0.5 mile until you pass a road on your left (3) which is part of Grizzly Trail. Continue on Coyote Trail for 0.7 mile until you pass the Marmot Trail turnoff on your left (2). Ski another 0.7 mile on Coyote Trail to the first trail junction (1) which you encountered at the beginning of the tour, and then continue for 0.2 mile to the trailhead.

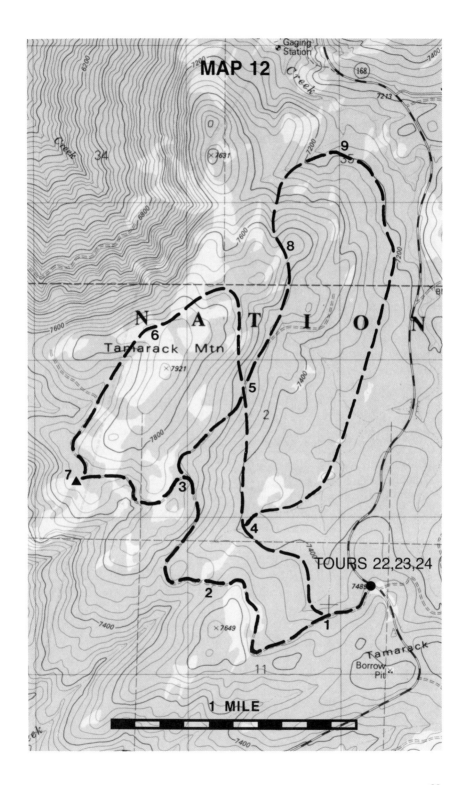

MAP 12

TOURS 22,23,24

1 MILE

# 24 Grizzly Trail Loop

MAP 12
PAGE 63

| | |
|---|---|
| Difficulty | 3 |
| Length | 6 miles round trip |
| Elevation | 7450/ + 700, − 700 |
| Navigation | Road, marked trail and map |
| Time | Most of a day |
| Season | Mid-December through mid-April |
| USGS topo | 15' series, Huntington Lake; 7.5' series, Huntington Lake |
| Start | Coyote Nordic Trailhead, 0.4 mile north of Tamarack Ridge Trailhead. |

Grizzly Trail Loop is the most difficult one of the tours which originate from Coyote Nordic Trailhead. This tour does not have the vistas which other tours in the area have but does take you over several miles of trail which are seldom used. These miles are also not as well-marked as the other trails in the area.

Begin the tour by skiing 0.2 mile southwest to a trail junction (1). Take the south (left) fork which is also known as Eagle Trail. Ski along this trail for 0.7 mile until you pass the Marmot Trail turnoff on your right (2).

Continue on Eagle Trail for 0.7 mile more to a road junction (3). Take the road to the north (right) which gradually descends for 0.5 mile until you cross Coyote Trail (5). You can also reach this point by following the Coyote Trail Loop tour.

After crossing Coyote Trail, continue to ski on the road for 0.6 mile until the road seems to disappear (8). Here you must descend 450' in 0.5 mile down a narrow gully. If you look hard, you may find some ribbons marking this gully but do not depend on them.

Shortly after the terrain levels at the bottom of the gully, you intersect a road (9). Turn south (right) onto this road and follow it for 1.8 miles back to Coyote Trail (4). In this section you want to head south, and you should ignore any signs which encourage you to turn away from that direction.

When you intersect Coyote Trail, follow it to the southeast (left) for about 50 yards until you pass the Marmot Trail turnoff on your right. Continue for 0.5 mile to the first trail junction (1) you encountered at the beginning of the tour. Finally, retrace your original route to the trailhead.

*Break in the clouds*

# 25 Chinese Peak and Red Mountain Plateau

MAP 13
PAGE 68

| | |
|---|---|
| Difficulty | 4 |
| Length | 8 miles round trip |
| Elevation | 7600/ + 1400, − 1400 |
| Navigation | Road, map and compass |
| Time | Full day |
| Season | Mid-December through April |
| USGS topo | 15′ series, Huntington Lake; 7.5′ series, Huntington Lake, Dogtooth Peak |
| Start | Highway 168, 1.1 miles southwest of Sierra Summit Ski Area and 0.2 mile southwest of where the highway crosses Coon Creek. |

This tour may be the finest backcountry trek in this area. To reach the plateau between Chinese Peak and Red Mountain you must climb steadily. Once at the plateau, enjoy your sense of accomplishment and celebrate with lunch at West Lake. The return descent on gentle slopes, which are sheltered from the sun, is another reward for your hard work.

Begin the tour with a search for the road which you will follow for a short distance before you head cross-country. You can locate this road on the south side of the highway, 0.2 mile southwest of the Coon Creek crossing. Park near Coon Creek and search for this road by skiing along the highway. If you choose to walk, be very cautious as the highway is narrow. Do not walk here when the highway is icy.

Now that you have overcome the first obstacle, ski east on the road for 0.2 mile to Coon Creek (1). You can also reach this point by a very steep but short climb along Coon Creek from the highway where you parked.

Cross Coon Creek on the road and immediately turn off the road. Ski south and then southeast; try to follow Coon Creek on its northeast side. You will probably cross a snow-covered road as you head toward an old cabin (2) located on the south side of Chinese Peak. The cabin is your only significant landmark along this stretch. It is therefore advisable to make frequent use of the map and a compass. From the cabin, ascend to Chinese Peak's southeast ridge (3).

From the ridge top, you generally head south. Ski over a small knob and then down to the base of the steepest section of the tour. Either climb directly up for 250′ to the top of a narrow ridge (4) or pick a roundabout route which ascends more gradually. The best view of Red Mountain for the entire trip is from this ridge and through the trees.

Continue by making a gentle arc to the south and east. Much of this final section is through dense trees. West Lake, the destination of this tour, is located at the very base of Red Mountain's west ridge. Just before you reach West Lake, you will encounter a clearing which you may confuse with the lake. West Lake is just ahead.

There are several possible extensions of this tour. If you are an expert skier you can ascend Red Mountain via the west ridge.

Another possibility is to circumnavigate Red Mountain. The loop around Red Mountain passes by Red and Strawberry Lakes, and adds an additional 4.0 miles and 650′ of elevation gain. Most of the loop is in the trees, but there are good views to the east and north from several points.

*Old cabin near Chinese Peak*

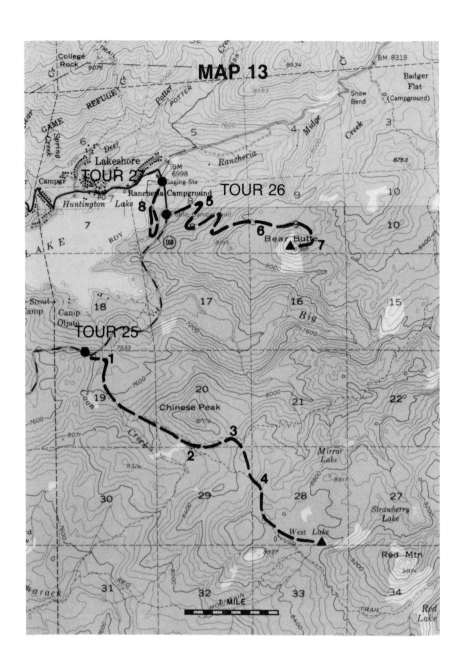

MAP 13
PAGE 68

# Bear Butte 26

| | |
|---|---|
| Difficulty | 3 |
| Length | 6 miles round trip |
| Elevation | 7150/ + 1450, − 1450 |
| Navigation | Road and map |
| Time | Most of a day |
| Season | December through April |
| USGS topo | 15′ series, Huntington Lake, Kaiser Peak; 7.5′ series, Huntington Lake, Kaiser Peak |
| Start | Highway 168 at the northeast end of Huntington Lake, 1.1 miles north of Sierra Summit Ski Area and 0.5 mile south of the Kaiser Pass turnoff. There is a turnout on the east side of the road. |

If you are using the 7.5′ series topos, you should note that "Bear Butte" is labeled "Black Butte" on the 1982 Huntington Lake topo. For traditional reasons, the name Bear Butte is used here.

Bear Butte, located just to the north of Sierra Summit Ski Area, is probably the easiest peak in the area to ascend on skis. Because the tour lies almost entirely on the north side of a ridge, the snow is often better here than elsewhere.

For most of its distance, this tour climbs steadily on a road; there is, however, 300′ of elevation gain just below the summit which is not on a road. This last section will give the advancing intermediate skier a small glimpse of what to expect on more difficult backcountry tours.

From the starting point, ski east on the road which climbs very gradually for 0.5 mile until you reach a road junction (5). The road you have been following continues straight for 0.5 mile to a dead end. Do not follow it; instead turn south (right) onto the intersecting road.

Follow this road as it climbs at a steep angle and zig-zags for 1.6 miles to a very large flat area (6) to the northwest of Bear Butte. Continue to ski east on the road, which stays level, until you reach a point just to the north of the peak.

From the north side of Bear Butte, continue skiing on the road which circles the peak and climbs to the saddle (7) located to the east of the peak. You must now climb directly to the summit. Near the top there is likely to be poor snow conditions such as windpack, ice, or bare spots. Be cautious.

The best route up Bear Butte is described above. For the return descent, most skiers may choose to follow the road the entire way. If you desire an alternative, you should retrace your route to the large flat area (6) to the northwest of Bear Butte. From the flat area, continue on the road for a short distance as it descends down a small gully. Once you leave the gully, you can also leave the road behind and enjoy a descent through the sparse, wooded terrain. Your route should cut across the zig-zags which you made while ascending.

*Getting air*

MAP 13
PAGE 68

Rancheria Trail **27**

| | |
|---|---|
| Difficulty | 1 |
| Length | 1 mile round trip |
| Elevation | 7000/ + 200, − 200 |
| Navigation | Road |
| Time | Short |
| Season | December through mid-April |
| USGS topo | 15′ series, Kaiser Peak, Huntington Lake |
| Start | Highway 168 at the northeast end of Huntington Lake, 0.1 mile south of the Kaiser Pass turnoff. |

This tour is by far the easiest beginner one in the Huntington and Shaver Lakes area. It follows the roads in Rancheria Campground which is adjacent to Huntington Lake. This small loop, which combines level areas with gradual ups and downs, offers good terrain for the first-time skier.

Ski south on the road which enters the campground for 0.3 mile until you encounter a road junction (**8**). Take the west (right) fork which takes you along the lake.

From the junction, ski for 0.3 mile to the halfway point of this tour. Here the road loops around, and you follow it back to the junction and to the starting point. You can also ski past the turnaround point, but expect to find yourself weaving through dense trees.

*Iced up*                    *Charlene Grandfield*

MAP **14**
PAGE 74

# Kaiser Pass and Luck Point

# 28

| | |
|---|---|
| Difficulty | 4 |
| Length | 16 miles round trip |
| Elevation | 7000/ + 2450, − 2450 |
| Navigation | Road and map |
| Time | Full day |
| Season | Mid-December through April |
| USGS topo | 15′ series, Kaiser Peak; 7.5′ series, Kaiser Peak, Mt. Givens |
| Start | Kaiser Pass turnoff on Highway 168 at the northeast end of Huntington Lake. |

The route described below follows Kaiser Pass Road for 6.5 miles to Kaiser Pass where it crosses the Kaiser Divide. While the area near the pass has a beautiful meadow from which to enjoy the ridges of Kaiser Divide, traveling an additional 1.5 miles brings you to the saddle to the north of Luck Point. The vistas toward Lake Thomas A. Edison and the Sierra Crest to the east are well worth this extra effort.

Even though the route climbs 2200′ before reaching Kaiser Pass, the gradient is never too steep because the road follows a circuitous route. In fact, the first 5.2 miles are so gradual that you may find the descent slower than you desire; however, the final 1.4 miles to the pass are steeper. If this section of narrow road has been packed by Southern California Edison's Sno-Cats or snowmobiles, you can expect a difficult descent.

Portal Powerhouse is located 0.1 mile northeast from Highway 168 on Kaiser Pass Road. The road is plowed for this short distance, and the tour actually begins here. From the powerhouse, it is easy to follow the main road despite several intersecting roads along the way.

From the powerhouse, ski on the road for 1.2 miles, as it parallels Rancheria Creek, to a sharp left turn **(1)**. The 1953 15′ topo shows the road continuing up the creek drainage, but the 1982 7.5′ topo shows the more recently realigned road.

Continue west on the road for 1.0 mile until it makes a sweeping turn to the right and heads back east. Along this last stretch there are good views of Huntington Lake. Since the tour is long, you may be returning to this section at sunset. Take a break then and enjoy the view.

From the turn, continue east for 0.3 mile to the Potter Pass Trail Cutoff **(2)** which leaves the main road. The Potter Pass tour leaves Kaiser Pass Road here. This tour to Luck Point continues on the main road.

Continue by skiing gradually uphill for 1.7 miles, and then continue for an additional 1.0 mile of level road. Here cross a drainage **(3)**, turn right with the road, and begin to climb at a steeper angle. Kaiser Pass **(4)** is

# 28

1.4 miles ahead.

Once at Kaiser Pass, continue on the road as it circles Kaiser Pass Meadow. After leaving the meadow, ski 0.3 mile north on the road. Just before the road begins to descend at a steeper angle (5), you must leave it.

From the road, traverse north and climb gradually for 0.4 mile until you reach a gully. Climb up the gully to the saddle north of Luck Point.

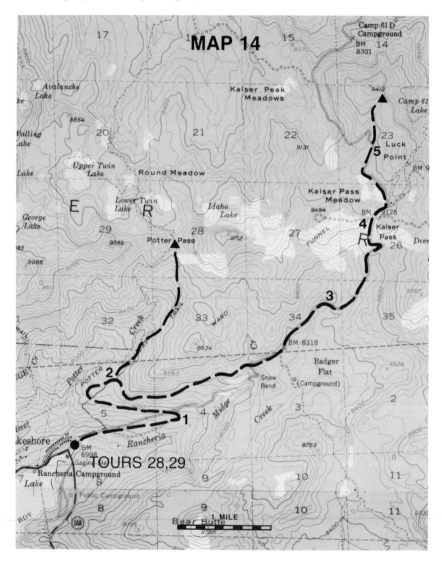

MAP **14**
PAGE 74

# Potter Pass **29**

| | |
|---|---|
| Difficulty | 4 |
| Length | 9 miles round trip |
| Elevation | 7000/ + 2000, − 2000 |
| Navigation | Road and map |
| Time | Full day |
| Season | Late December through mid-April |
| USGS topo | 15' series, Kaiser Peak; 7.5' series, Kaiser Peak |
| Start | Kaiser Pass turnoff on Highway 168 at the northeast end of Huntington Lake. |

The views from Potter Pass are undoubtedly the best of any tour in this area. Be sure to do this one on a clear day so that you can enjoy the spectacular scenery to both the north and south. By the time you reach the pass, Huntington Lake will be 2000' below, all the work will be over, and you can savor views of Chinese Peak and Red Mountain to the south and the impressive Sierra Crest to the north. Mt. Ritter and Banner Peak, located at the north end of the Minarets Wilderness, are the two peaks visible far to the north.

Your first objective is to reach the Potter Pass Trail Cutoff (**2**) which is located 2.5 miles from the starting point. Refer to the Kaiser Pass and Luck Point tour (no. 28) for directions to this point.

At the cutoff, leave the main road and head north on a minor road. Soon this road will disappear, and you will need to pick your own route. At first you will find it easier to ski on the west side of Potter Creek. If you choose that route, you will have to drop down to and cross the creek before it hems you in against the steep cliffs. That route is not recommended.

A better alternative is to begin on the east side of Potter Creek. This route avoids several potentially difficult creek crossings but requires picking a route through dense trees at the beginning. Ski northeast and parallel to Potter Creek for 0.4 mile and then veer away from the creek. Continue by climbing at a steep angle to the north toward the southwest facing slopes to the south of Potter Pass. Exercise caution in the open areas just south of the pass as they are avalanche prone.

Once at Potter Pass, relax and enjoy your accomplishment. If you still have energy, tackle the northern slopes which invite you to cut some turns. These slopes lead down to a meadow and Twin Lakes.

From Potter Pass, be sure to make the short climb to the high point west of the pass. The rocks make an ideal place for lunch, and the views are better than from the pass.

# 30 Huntington Lake

MAP 15
PAGE 77

| | |
|---|---|
| Difficulty | 1–2 |
| Length | Up to 11 miles round trip |
| Elevation | 6950/Up to +450, −450 |
| Navigation | Road and/or map |
| Time | Up to full day |
| Season | Mid-December through mid-April |
| USGS topo | 15' series, Kaiser Peak, Huntington Lake |
| Start | The northeast end of Huntington Lake where Huntington Lake Road is not plowed. This point is 0.4 mile west of the Kaiser Pass turnoff. |

This tour is on snow-covered Huntington Lake Road. It is a good trip if you want to cover lots of miles without worrying about route-finding.

From the starting point, you can ski west on the road for 5.3 miles to the dam at the southwest end of the lake. Unfortunately, this road is also used by snowmobilers. As an alternative, you may want to ski right along the lake shore from the starting point.

If you choose to ski along the shore, you can either return along that same route or on the road. In the latter case, your best bet is to follow one of the subdivision roads from the lake to Huntington Lake Road.

*Huntington Lake from Potter Pass*

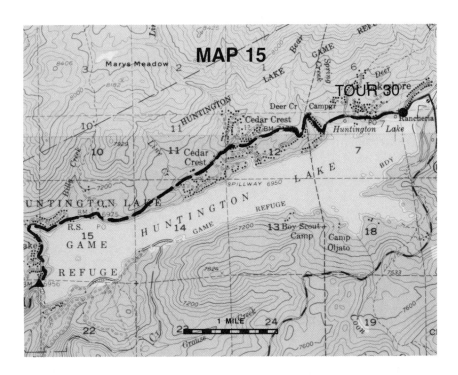

*North from Potter Pass*

*High Sierra from Buck Rock*

# Kings Canyon

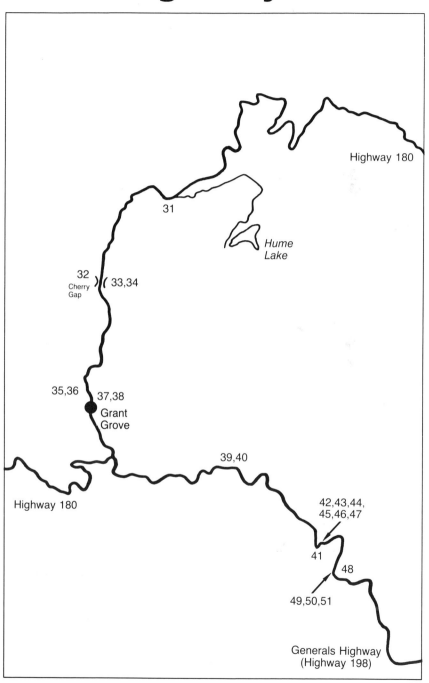

Highway 180

31

Hume
Lake

32
Cherry
Gap

33,34

35,36

37,38
Grant
Grove

39,40

Highway 180

42,43,44,
45,46,47

41

48

49,50,51

Generals Highway
(Highway 198)

# 31 Indian Basin

MAP 16
PAGE 80

| | |
|---|---|
| Difficulty | 1 |
| Length | Short |
| Elevation | 5850/Nil |
| Navigation | Adjacent to road |
| Time | Short |
| Season | Late December through March |
| USGS topo | 15' series, Tehipite Dome |
| Start | Highway 180, 6.0 miles north of Grant Grove. |

Except for the problem of low elevation, Indian Basin is probably the best spot for first-time skiers who desire a large, flat, and open area to practice. The meadow is large, and you can follow Indian Creek southwest for more than a mile before the trees become a problem. You can also explore the woods to the northwest.

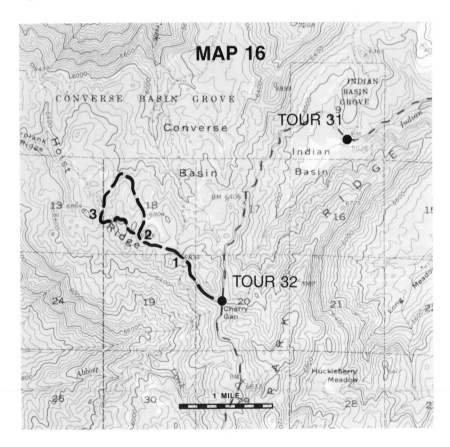

MAP 16
PAGE 80

# Chicago Stump Loop 32

| | |
|---|---|
| Difficulty | 2 |
| Length | 5 miles round trip |
| Elevation | 6800/ + 400, − 400 |
| Navigation | Road |
| Time | Half day |
| Season | Mid-December through early April |
| USGS topo | 15′ series, Tehipite Dome |
| Start | West side of Highway 180 at Cherry Gap, 3.0 miles north of Grant Grove. |

There is a lot to say about this tour, and it is all good. The route is along easy, rolling terrain with only a few hills. All along the route you will have good views, and after the first 0.7 mile, you will find countless places to play. The area also has an interesting history. The only possible drawback is that the road is marked for snowmobile use. Luckily, experience shows that this is not a popular place for them.

Ski to the northwest on the road which traverses the hillside for 0.7 mile to a saddle (1). Along this section, to the southwest, you will see what remains of a grand grove of mature sequoias. In the late 1800's, this area was logged to supply lumber to build the flume which carried even more lumber to Sanger. Following this initial devastation, the area's second growth was wiped out by the great McGee fire of 1955. Today, a third growth has taken hold after the planting of four million saplings.

Cross the saddle and continue on the main road to the northwest. The main road should be obvious since it remains level while the roads to the north and south drop at a steep angle. From the saddle, ski 0.3 mile until you encounter a flat area. Ski another 0.3 mile until you reach a road junction (2) which is the beginning of a loop.

At the junction, take the fork which heads north (right). If the snow is old, it is better to ski the loop in this direction. While skiing around the loop, you will pass countless stumps, many of which have been blackened by fire. There will also be some beautiful mature sequoias.

Eventually, you turn south with the road as it leads you to another road junction (3). About 100 yards before you reach this junction, you should see a sign indicating that the Chicago Stump is located 100 yards off the road to the east (left). If the snow is not too deep, you can find the sign at the base of the burned stump which tells the story about the great "California Hoax."

Apparently, an enterprising person realized that a tree the size of a giant sequoia was beyond belief to most people. So he cut one off at 50 feet, then hollowed out the stump, and finally cut the stump into sections. The sections were reassembled at the 1893 World's Columbian Exposition in Chicago where few who saw it believed it was real. The cut tree was the General Noble Tree and its blackened stump reminds us that our curiosity occasionally leads to destruction. Unfortunately, this tree can never be replaced. So, let us hope that our curiosity about it and other wilderness monuments encourages us to promote forest management and protect the environment rather than destroy it.

At the road junction (**3**) near the Chicago Stump, you can make a sharp turn to the north (right) onto Hoist Road. You can follow it for 0.5 mile or more before the snow becomes sparse.

To reach the end from the junction (**3**), follow the main road south for less than 0.1 mile until you pass a road on your right marked Verplank Trail. Continue to follow the main road in a southeasterly direction as it climbs over a small hill and drops down to the loop's starting point (**2**). Now you simply retrace your route to the start of the tour.

*Carving turns*                                                                 *Gary Schaezlein*

MAP **17**
PAGE 84

**Cherry Gap to
Indian Basin** **33**

| | |
|---|---|
| Difficulty | 2 |
| Length | 3 miles one-way to Indian Basin or up to 6 miles round trip |
| Elevation | 6800/ − 950 one-way or 6800/Up to + 950, − 950 round trip |
| Navigation | Road |
| Time | Few hours to half day |
| Season | Mid-December through early April |
| USGS topo | 15′ series, Tehipite Dome |
| Start | East side of Highway 180 at Cherry Gap, 3.0 miles north of Grant Grove. |
| End | Same as starting point for round trip or Indian Basin on Highway 180, 6.0 miles north of Grant Grove for one-way trip. |

If you only have a half day and want to cover several miles quickly, this tour is an excellent choice. The tour is easy to follow, descends steadily for 3.0 miles, and offers you a choice of either a one-way or round trip tour.

From the starting point, ski east on the snow-covered road. Almost immediately, you will encounter a road junction. The south (right) fork is part of the Cherry Gap Loop tour. For this tour, take the north (left) fork. Continue to ski northeast on the road for 3.0 miles, or as far as you desire, and then turn around.

To make a one-way tour, ski on the road until you reach a plowed road, the road from Highway 180 to Hume Lake. From this point you must walk 0.6 mile west (left) to Highway 180 where the one-way tour ends at Indian Basin.

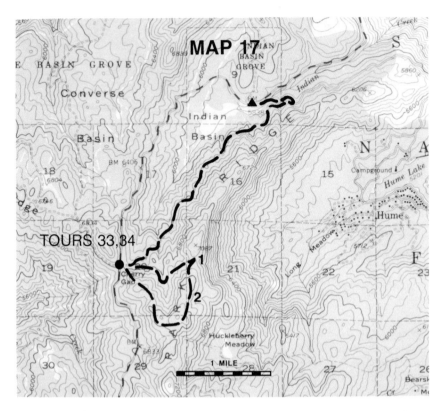

MAP 17

TOURS 33,84

*Solitude in the High Sierra*

MAP 17
PAGE 84

# Cherry Gap Loop **34**

| | |
|---|---|
| Difficulty | 2−4 |
| Length | 3 miles round trip |
| Elevation | 6800/ + 500, − 500 |
| Navigation | Road, marked trail and map |
| Time | Few hours |
| Season | Mid-December through early April |
| USGS topo | 15′ series, Tehipite Dome |
| Start | East side of Highway 180 at Cherry Gap, 3.0 miles north of Grant Grove. |

This loop is quite difficult due to one very steep section. This tour becomes much easier if you omit that section. If you choose to omit it, you will have to retrace your steps, but you can still fully enjoy this area.

From the starting point, ski east on the snow-covered road for a very short distance until you encounter a road junction. The north (left) fork is part of the Cherry Gap to Indian Basin tour. For this tour, take the south (right) fork and ski until you reach a saddle **(1)**. You are now 1.1 miles from the start and have completed the easiest section of the tour.

From the saddle, follow the road which heads south (right), and climb for 0.3 mile to a ridge top where the road disappears.

On the ridge top, locate the marked trail and follow it south along the east side of the ridge for 0.2 mile to a spot with an excellent view to the east **(2)**. This viewpoint is a good destination for intermediate skiers.

If you are continuing on the loop, ski south for 0.3 mile more. Now you turn west (right) and ski along the south side of two high points for 0.3 mile. Finally, you turn northwest (right) and follow a ridge for 0.8 mile back to the starting point. You will find the very last 0.2 mile which descends 250′ the most difficult stretch of the entire loop.

# 35 North Grove Loop

MAP 18
PAGE 88

| | |
|---|---|
| Difficulty | 3 |
| Length | 2 miles round trip |
| Elevation | 6400/+450, −450 |
| Navigation | Road |
| Time | Few hours |
| Season | December through early April |
| USGS topo | 15′ series, Giant Forest, Tehipite Dome |
| Start | General Grant Tree parking area. Drive 0.2 mile north on Highway 180 from Grant Grove. Turn west (left) onto the road which winds for 0.9 mile to the parking area. |

This short tour takes you through a beautiful grove of giant sequoias, but don't let the shortness deceive you since both the downhill and the uphill sections are steep. Also, the snow quality deteriorates very rapidly, even after a snowfall, due to icy ruts created by skiers and holes created by hikers. Consider doing this tour only when conditions are ideal.

Locate the marked road at the west (lower) end of the parking area which leads west to the North Grove. Ski down the road for 0.2 mile to a road junction (1). The best direction to ski the loop, which starts and ends here, is clockwise. By starting on the south (left) fork, you climb up the steepest section which is also the narrowest and curviest part of the loop. This uphill section may also contain some bad gullies created by water which would be hazardous to a skier heading downhill.

One final note about the junction (1): If you are going fast when you approach it, you may unknowingly pass it by, but don't worry since you will be skiing the south (left) fork.

From the junction (1), ski down the road as it winds through the forest for 0.4 mile until you encounter another junction (2). The road to the south (left) leads to Sequoia Lake which, due to its elevation of 5280′, is a poor destination. Instead, take the north (right) fork and follow it as it winds and descends for 0.5 mile until you reach the lowest point on the tour. Near here you will pass the Millwood fire road on your left.

Continue on the road which now climbs at a very steep angle back to the first junction (1). Finally, retrace your tracks to the starting point.

*Springtime outfit*

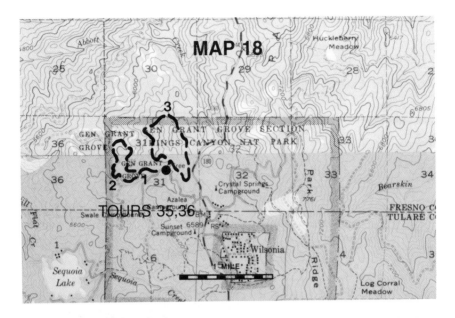

*Birthday party in a tent*                    Lee Griffith

MAP 18
PAGE 88

# Bridle Trail Loop 36

| | |
|---|---|
| Difficulty | 3 |
| Length | 2 miles round trip |
| Elevation | 6400/ + 300, − 300 |
| Navigation | Marked trail |
| Time | Few hours |
| Season | Late December through March |
| USGS topo | 15′ series, Giant Forest, Tehipite Dome |
| Start | General Grant Tree parking area. Drive 0.2 mile north on Highway 180 from Grant Grove. Turn west (left) onto the road which winds for 0.9 mile to the parking area. |

This tour takes you through a variety of wooded terrain as it meanders through the Grant Grove area. Because the tour contains many steep, narrow trails, it is more difficult than you might expect.

From the parking area, hike or ski on the obvious path to the historic Gamlin Cabin which is located very close to the General Grant Tree. Leave the path and ski past the cabin for 50 yards until you intersect the summer equestrian trail. This trail forms the Bridle Trail Loop tour. I suggest that you ski the loop in a counterclockwise direction as described below.

Ski southeast (right) along the trail. You should follow the markers very carefully because the trail is not obvious in places. In 0.3 mile, you turn north and shortly reach the stables. Continue to climb and pass to the east (right) of a high point.

After you pass the high point, you start to descend gradually until you reach the north boundary of Kings Canyon National Park (3). Here, turn southwest (left) and continue along the trail. After descending for 0.2 mile, you must look carefully for the point where the trail turns south (left).

As the trail weaves to the south, you will encounter the most difficult skiing. At the point where the route begins to climb, you are only 0.3 mile from the junction near Gamlin Cabin.

# 37 Panoramic Point and Park Ridge Lookout

MAP 19
PAGE 93

| | |
|---|---|
| Difficulty | 3 |
| Length | 4 miles round trip to Panoramic Point or 9 miles round trip to Park Ridge Lookout |
| Elevation | 6600/+750, −750 to Panoramic Point or 6600/ +1000, −1000 to Park Ridge Lookout |
| Navigation | Road |
| Time | Half day to full day |
| Season | Mid-December through early April |
| USGS topo | 15' series, Giant Forest, Tehipite Dome |
| Start | Grant Grove Visitor Center. |

To reach both Panoramic Point and Park Ridge Lookout, which are located on Park Ridge, you must climb steadily for the first 2.0 miles. The ridge runs north and south, and drops to the east and west. The steepness of the ridge accentuates the spectacular views of Kings Canyon and Sequoia National Parks, and the surrounding areas. To the east, forests separate you from the high granite peaks of the Sierra Crest, many of which are over 13,000'. To the west are the forests and beyond is the Central Valley.

The best time to ski this tour is immediately after a snowfall. The route to Park Ridge, described below, is on its west side and is subjected daily to thawing and freezing. These factors combine to create poor conditions for such a steep decent. You may find the descent described in the Park Ridge to Upper Bearskin Creek tour easier but the route is not as straightforward.

To reach the snow-covered road which this tour follows, walk 0.2 mile east and then north on the plowed road from the visitor center at Grant Grove.

Ski up the snow-covered road for 0.2 mile until you pass a road on your right. Ski another 0.4 mile, and you will see a marker which indicates that the ski touring trail leaves the road to the right and heads up a gully. You can follow either the trail or the road since the trail shortly intersects the road again.

Continuing on the road from the point where the trail leaves the road, ski for 100 yards until you encounter a road junction (1). The fork to the north (left) dead-ends almost immediately, and you should take the fork to the east (right). Ski ahead for 0.1 mile until the marked trail intersects the road again.

From this intersection, ski on the road for another 0.4 mile to Round Meadow which is located on the west (left) side of the road. The meadow is a pleasant rest stop.

From Round Meadow, follow the road for 0.7 mile to another road junction (**2**). Here you must choose whether your destination is Panoramic Point or Park Ridge Lookout. You may well decide to visit both spots since you are close to the ridge top where both are located.

**Panoramic Point.** To reach Panoramic Point, continue north (straight) for 0.1 mile until you reach the end of the road. Locate the ski touring markers and climb, as you follow them, for 0.2 mile to Panoramic Point.

**Park Ridge Lookout.** To reach Park Ridge Lookout, at the junction (**2**) take the road to the northeast (right) which gradually turns south. Follow this road as it traverses Park Ridge on its west side for 1.4 miles until you come to a saddle (**3**). From the saddle, follow the road as it crosses the ridge to its east side and continue to traverse south for 1.4 miles to Park Ridge Lookout.

You can also take an alternate route from Panoramic Point to Park Ridge Lookout which almost completely avoids the road. Ski along the ridge top and follow the summer trail from Panoramic Point. Cross the road at the saddle (**3**), intersect the road again 0.2 mile north of the lookout, and then follow the road to the lookout. Skiing along this alternate route is definitely more difficult than skiing on the road.

*Late afternoon descent*                    *Kim Grandfield*

# 38 Park Ridge to Upper Bearskin Creek

MAP 19
PAGE 93

| | |
|---|---|
| Difficulty | 3 |
| Length | 9 or 12 miles one-way |
| Elevation | 6600/+1500, −1200 for 9 mile tour and 6600/ +1850, −1550 for 12 mile tour |
| Navigation | Road, marked trail and map |
| Time | Full day |
| Season | Mid-December through early April |
| USGS topo | 15' series, Giant Forest, Tehipite Dome |
| Start | Grant Grove Visitor Center. |
| End | Quail Flat which is located on Generals Highway (Highway 198) 3.7 miles east of the junction of Highway 180 and Generals Highway. |

You will undoubtedly find that this tour is one of the best in the Kings Canyon area. By combining the Panoramic Point and Park Ridge Lookout tour with the Upper Bearskin Creek tour, you can enjoy the variety of two separate tours without retracing your tracks. You also avoid the some-times treacherous descent from Park Ridge back to the visitor center at Grant Grove.

Your first objective in this tour is to reach Park Ridge Lookout (5). You should refer to the Panoramic Point and Park Ridge Lookout tour (no. 37) description for directions.

After you have enjoyed the views from the lookout, backtrack on the road for 0.8 mile. You should be looking for a point (4), almost directly north of which there is a gully which begins 200' below the road. Be aware that the correct gully has a ridge to its east which separates it from another gully.

Leave the road and ski towards the gully for 0.3 mile until you reach the top of it. At the top of the gully, look for the road which descends along the east (right) side of it. Follow this road as it descends for 0.4 mile until you intersect another road (6). The road you intersect is part of the Upper Bearskin Creek tour.

At the road junction, you have two alternatives. The shortest is to head directly to Quail Flat and the end of the tour. Turn east (right) and follow the Upper Bearskin Creek tour (no. 40) in reverse.

The longer alternative is to turn west (left) and ski to the vista point as described in the Upper Bearskin Creek tour. After savoring the view, fol-low the Upper Bearskin Creek tour back to Quail Flat. This alternative is longer than the first by 2.6 miles, and you have an additional elevation change of +350', −350'.

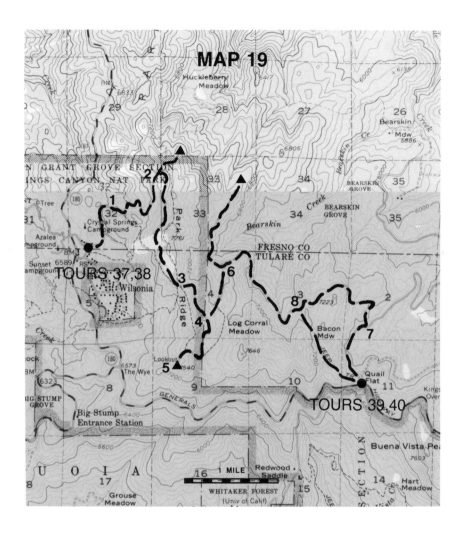

# 39 Quail Flat Loop

| | |
|---|---|
| Difficulty | 3 |
| Length | 3 miles round trip |
| Elevation | 6900/+450, −450 |
| Navigation | Road and marked trail |
| Time | Few hours |
| Season | Mid-December through mid-April |
| USGS topo | 15′ series, Giant Forest |
| Start | Quail Flat which is located on Generals Highway (Highway 198) 3.7 miles east of the junction of Highway 180 and Generals Highway. |

This loop, which circles Peak 7223, is an excellent short excursion. From the peak's north side, you have excellent views 4000′ down into the Kings River drainage.

You can ski this loop in either direction; the counterclockwise direction ends with a descent through a less-traveled area and is described below.

There are four snow-covered roads which leave the starting point. One road leaves from the east side of the parking area, two roads leave from the north side, and one road leaves from the west side. As you face the two roads heading north, take the one on the left. The loop returns to this point on the road which leaves from the west side of the parking area. This road is a little difficult to see from the parking area, but both roads used in this tour are marked ski touring trails.

Ski on the road which heads north and descend gradually for 0.7 mile to a road junction **(7)**. The fork to the northeast (straight) eventually leads to Hume Lake; instead take the fork to the north (left) and immediately start to climb.

After climbing for 0.9 mile and 250′ you level off as the road rounds the north side of Peak 7223. While enjoying the views, continue on the road for 0.6 mile until you reach a gully **(8)** on the west side of the peak. The road crosses the gully and continues to Bearskin Creek while the Quail Flat Loop turns south and heads up the gully. The turnoff point and the route up the gully are marked.

From the road, ski south up the gully for 0.2 mile and 150′ to a saddle where you intersect a road. Follow the road south along the west (right) side of the drainage. As you descend, the road becomes steeper, and the final 0.4 mile of the tour descends along a ridge to the southeast. If it is late in the day when you ski the final stretch, you may find the sun peering at you through the trees. Savor the beauty and serenity of the scene.

MAP **19**
PAGE 93

# Upper Bearskin Creek **40**

| | |
|---|---|
| Difficulty | 3 |
| Length | 9 miles round trip |
| Elevation | 6900/+1400, −1400 |
| Navigation | Road and marked trail |
| Time | Full day |
| Season | Mid-December through mid-April |
| USGS topo | 15' series, Giant Forest, Tehipite Dome |
| Start | Quail Flat which is located on Generals Highway (Highway 198) 3.7 miles east of the junction of Highway 180 and Generals Highway. |

The Upper Bearskin Creek tour is an extension of the Quail Flat Loop tour. This 2.8 mile extension takes you on an easy-to-follow road to an overlook point where you can view the spectacular Kings River canyon. Here, you can appreciate the Rodgers Ridge and Tombstone Ridge skyline and the unusual granite spire named Obelisk.

The first 2.2 miles of this tour are identical to the Quail Flat Loop tour (no. 39). Follow those directions to reach the gully (**8**) west of Peak 7223.

For the Upper Bearskin Creek tour, cross the gully and continue on the road for 1.0 mile until you pass a road on your right. Continue to ski for another 0.5 mile until you reach a road junction (**6**). The road to the south (left) is part of the Park Ridge to Upper Bearskin Creek tour. This tour continues to the west (straight).

From the junction, ski for 0.3 mile until you cross a drainage which is the upper end of Bearskin Creek. Continue to ski north for 0.7 mile until you find yourself in an open area on a ridge. Just ahead you will drop at a steep angle for a short distance, and 0.3 mile from the open spot you will come to a prominent point. You can recognize this spot by the spectacular views and by noting that the road leaves the ridge here and descends to the northwest. This prominent point is the destination of this tour.

For the return trip, retrace your tracks to the gully (**8**) which is on the Quail Flat Loop tour. Once you are back to that point you should complete the Quail Flat Loop tour by heading south up the gully as described in the Quail Flat Loop tour.

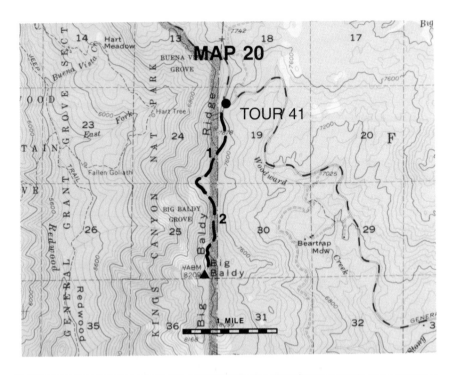

*Break time*

MAP 20
PAGE 96

# Big Baldy  41

| | |
|---|---|
| Difficulty | 3 |
| Length | 4 miles round trip |
| Elevation | 7600/ + 1000, − 1000 |
| Navigation | Marked trail |
| Time | Half day |
| Season | Mid-December through mid-April |
| USGS topo | 15′ series, Giant Forest |
| Start | Generals Highway (Highway 198), 6.8 miles southeast of the junction of Highway 180 and Generals Highway. There is a parking area 0.1 mile farther east. |

This tour is short, but challenging, and rewards you with 360 degrees of incomparable views. The tour takes you along the crest of Big Baldy Ridge where the views come and go as the route passes through clear and wooded areas. Once at the summit of Big Baldy, you can look down on the rich agricultural San Joaquin Valley to the west. To the north, east, and south lie the backcountry of Sierra and Sequoia National Forests, and Kings Canyon and Sequoia National Parks. A particularly prominent landmark is Buck Rock to the north. All in all, the views are truly spectacular.

The route which follows Big Baldy Ridge south from Generals Highway is well-marked with yellow triangles. It climbs and drops as it crosses back and forth across the crest of the ridge. The steepest section is the last 0.5 mile to the summit.

Leave the highway and head south by following the markers which lead you on a traverse around the east side of Peak 7878. As you traverse, you climb to the crest of the ridge **(1)** on the south side of the peak. Note that the ski trail does not follow the hiking trail which is located to the west of the peak.

From the crest, ski for 0.3 mile farther south along the ridge, and then climb and traverse around the west side of a knob. Once around the knob, you ski downhill to a saddle **(2)** on the ridge.

From this saddle, you continue south and shortly you will find that the marked trail climbs steeply to the summit. You approach the actual summit from the northeast since the west is a shear rocky cliff.

If the trail to Big Baldy is in poor shape, icy, or rutted, you may want to return via an alternate route. To do so, ski north back to the highway by making a track below the ridge, and parallel to and east of the marked trail. You may find better conditions here.

| | |
|---|---|
| Difficulty | 2 |
| Length | 3 miles round trip |
| Elevation | 7550/ + 200, − 200 |
| Navigation | Road and map |
| Time | Few hours |
| Season | December through April |
| USGS topo | 15′ series, Giant Forest |
| Start | Big Meadows Trailhead which is located at the junction of Generals Highway (Highway 198) and the road to Big Meadows. The road to Big Meadows is on the north side of the highway and 7.0 miles southeast of the junction of Highway 180 and Generals Highway. Park either at the very start of the tour or 0.1 mile west. |

If you are a novice skier, you will find this tour to Rabbit Meadow an excellent choice. The meadow is a quiet, secluded place where you will be away from the large number of skiers who use the road to Big Meadows. On the other hand, if you are looking for a longer tour, you may want to consider the one to Big Meadows.

In the area of the starting point, you will often find tracks going in every direction. This tour follows the road heading north from the starting point, and you should have no trouble recognizing it. If in doubt, take your time and make sure.

From the starting point, ski for 0.2 mile until you pass markers on your right which mark the Starlight Trail. Continue on the road for 0.6 mile to a road junction (1). The sign indicates that Rabbit Meadow is to the northwest (left) and Big Meadows is to the east (right).

Ski on the road toward Rabbit Meadow for 100 yards until you reach another junction. Here, take the north (right) fork and ski for 0.3 mile until you come to Rabbit Meadow which is on the east (right) side of the road. From the meadow, you can retrace your route to the start or make a small loop around it.

To make the loop, continue north on the road as it parallels Rabbit Meadow. Ski 0.1 mile past the meadow and turn south with the road. Continue following the road for 0.5 mile until you intersect the main road to Big Meadows (2). Although the road may not be distinct along parts of this last 0.5 mile, follow the most obvious, clear, and level route.

Once you are back on the main road, ski west (right) for 0.2 mile to the junction (1) where you turned off to Rabbit Meadow. Now, retrace your route to the starting point.

*Slow going with a heavy pack*

# 43 Big Meadows

MAP 21
PAGE 101

| | |
|---|---|
| Difficulty | 2 |
| Length | 7 miles round trip |
| Elevation | 7550/ + 350, − 350 |
| Navigation | Road |
| Time | Most of a day |
| Season | December through April |
| USGS topo | 15′ series, Giant Forest |
| Start | Big Meadows Trailhead which is located at the junction of Generals Highway (Highway 198) and the road to Big Meadows. The road to Big Meadows is on the north side of the highway and 7.0 miles southeast of the junction of Highway 180 and Generals Highway. Park either at the very start of the tour or 0.1 mile west. |

The tour to Big Meadows is the most popular tour in this area. There is a warming hut at the meadows which is operated by Wilsonia Ski Touring. Once there, you can explore countless places including the far reaches of this irregularly shaped meadow, Buck Rock, and Weaver Lake. Tours to Buck Rock and Weaver Lake are described elsewhere in this guidebook.

From the starting point, ski north on the snow-covered road for 0.8 mile to a road junction (1). The sign there indicates that Rabbit Meadow is to the northwest (left). Ski east (right) for 0.3 mile to the crest in the road. Continue for another 0.1 mile until you encounter a road junction (3) not shown on the 15′ series topo.

Take the fork which descends to the east (right) and ski for 1.5 miles until you reach the very north edge of a large but narrow meadow. This meadow is one of the arms of Big Meadows.

Continue for 0.1 mile until you reach a fork (4) in the road. The west (left) fork leads to Buck Rock; instead you should ski on the east (right) fork for 0.4 mile until the road passes near a large section of Big Meadows. To reach the meadows, ski south (right) for a short distance through some trees. Once in the meadow you will see several cabins; the newest-looking one is the warming hut.

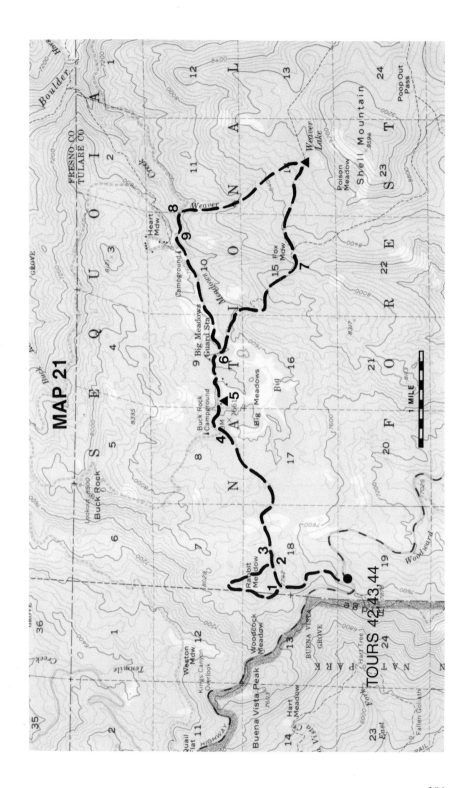

MAP 21

TOURS 42, 43, 44

MAP 21
PAGE 101

# 44 Weaver Lake

| | |
|---|---|
| Difficulty | 4 |
| Length | 14 miles round trip |
| Elevation | 7550/ + 1450, − 1450 |
| Navigation | Road, map and compass |
| Time | Full day |
| Season | December through April |
| USGS topo | 15′ series, Giant Forest |
| Start | Big Meadows Trailhead which is located at the junction of Generals Highway (Highway 198) and the road to Big Meadows. The road to Big Meadows is on the north side of the highway and 7.0 miles southeast of the junction of Highway 180 and Generals Highway. Park either at the very start of the tour or 0.1 mile west. |

The tour to Weaver Lake is an excellent choice if you are seeking some adventure in the Big Meadows area of Kings Canyon. Aside from challenging backcountry skiing this tour offers both beauty and solitude. Surrounded by sheer cliffs, the lake, which is rarely visited in winter, sits at the base of Shell Mountain.

The first half of the tour to Weaver Lake is the same as the tour to Big Meadows. Refer to the Big Meadows tour (no. 43) description for directions to the meadows (5). If you stop at the warming hut, the first thing you must do is return to the road.

Ski east on the road for 0.2 mile until you reach a narrow arm of Big Meadows. Continue on the road for 0.1 mile as it turns northeast and parallels the east (right) side of the meadow. Ski another 0.1 mile on the road to Big Meadows Guard Station. Continue 0.1 mile farther and reach the point where you leave the road (6). At this point, you can see a clearing to the southeast and below which is also part of Big Meadows.

From the point where you leave the road, you can see Shell Mountain in the background to the southeast. Between here and Weaver Lake, you can only see it occasionally; so, do not depend on it as a landmark. You will need to refer to the topo and a compass since the route is not marked and the hiking trail which the route follows will be difficult to discern.

Leave the road, drop down to the meadow, and then ski southeast. There will be a ridge to your south, and you must start to traverse southeast and around it, and climb. You should turn south and ski up a gully to the east of the ridge. When you are about 0.3 mile up, cross the gully and climb at a steep angle to the southeast once again. As the route becomes less steep, you will pass to the northeast of a knob and then drop down to a saddle where small Fox Meadow (7) is located.

## 44

From Fox Meadow, ascend at a very steep angle to the east for 0.2 mile. As the slope becomes less steep, you may find the Weaver Lake-Jennie Lake summer trail junction. Continue climbing gradually and predominantly east for 1.0 mile until you reach Weaver Lake. Once at the lake, be aware of avalanche danger from the steep cliffs of Shell Mountain.

To return, you can either retrace your route to Weaver Lake or descend along Weaver Creek. The distance back to Big Meadows Guard Station is approximately the same via either route. Be aware though that the Weaver Creek route drops 1100′ in half the distance it takes the other route to drop the same elevation. Due to the steep descent, the creek route is obviously more difficult.

To return via Weaver Creek, ski north from the outlet of the lake. Follow the drainage by staying on its west (left) side. You will find that the first 0.5 mile descends slowly, but the next 1.0 mile through trees is very steep. By skiing parallel to the creek, you will eventually intersect the road **(8)** which leads to Horse Corral Meadow.

Once you are on the road, ski west (left) and note that the road you pass on your left is not on the topo. Continue to and cross Big Meadows Creek. Shortly after, you will reach a road junction **(9)**.

At the junction, ski west (left) for 1.5 miles to the Big Meadows Guard Station. Now it is a simple matter to continue on the road and follow your original route back to the starting point.

*Buck Rock*

# 45 Buck Rock

MAP 22
PAGE 105

| | |
|---|---|
| Difficulty | 3 |
| Length | 8 to 10 miles round trip |
| Elevation | 7550/+800, −800 via Horse Flat Trail or 7550/ +1100, −1100 via Buck Rock Trail |
| Navigation | Road and map via Horse Flat Trail or road via Buck Rock Trail |
| Time | Full day |
| Season | December through April |
| USGS topo | 15′ series, Giant Forest |
| Start | Big Meadows Trailhead which is located at the junction of Generals Highway (Highway 198) and the road to Big Meadows. The road to Big Meadows is on the north side of the highway and 7.0 miles southeast of the junction of Highway 180 and Generals Highway. Park either at the very start of the tour or 0.1 mile west. |

Impressive is the only word for the lookout atop Buck Rock. Like a giant thumb, this rock rises 150′ above the trail and drops even farther to the northwest. As you approach this interesting sculpture, you may wonder how you can reach the very top. As you examine it closer, you can see the erector set-like staircase scaling the rock, the gate to which is unfortunately locked. Regardless, with its many spectacular views, the tour to Buck Rock is still worth a good day's workout.

The tour description below includes two standard routes to Buck Rock. A third, more adventuresome route called the Buck Rock via Ridge tour, is described elsewhere.

The Buck Rock Trail is the easiest to follow because it is entirely on a road. It is also the longest route at 5.0 miles one-way. The Horse Flat Trail is only 3.7 miles one-way, but there is one 0.4 mile portion which does not follow a road. If you can read a topographic map, you should have little trouble with the Horse Flat Trail, although you should note that it is a little more difficult to follow when returning from Buck Rock.

From the trailhead, follow the snow-covered road north for 0.8 mile to a road junction (1). Rabbit Meadow is to the northwest (left); you want the fork to the east (right). Ski east for 0.3 mile to the crest of the road and continue for 0.1 mile until you reach another road junction (2). The Horse Flat and Buck Rock Trails separate here.

**Buck Rock Trail.** The Buck Rock Trail follows the road to the east (right). Ski on this road for 1.6 miles to a road junction (3). The fork to the northeast (right) leads to Big Meadows. You should take the fork to the north (left) and follow this road as it climbs gradually but continuously.

## 45

From the junction, ski for 1.2 miles until you pass the intersection (**4**) of the Horse Flat Trail and the Buck Rock Trail. This intersection is not marked.

Continue on the road for 0.5 mile until you pass to the west of a small knob. Here, you will get your first view of Buck Rock. Ski on the road for another 0.4 mile to the east side of another knob. Here, the main road turns east (right); instead you should ski northwest (left) on a lesser road until you reach the base of Buck Rock.

**Horse Flat Trail.** From the junction (**2**), the Horse Flat Trail follows the road to the north (left). Ski on this road as it ascends along a gully for 0.6 mile. Follow the road as it crosses the head of the gully and continue to the northeast for 0.5 mile to its end (**5**).

At the end of the road, you should pick a route and ski to the northeast for 0.4 mile to the intersection with the Buck Rock Trail (**4**). From here, follow the Buck Rock Trail route to Buck Rock.

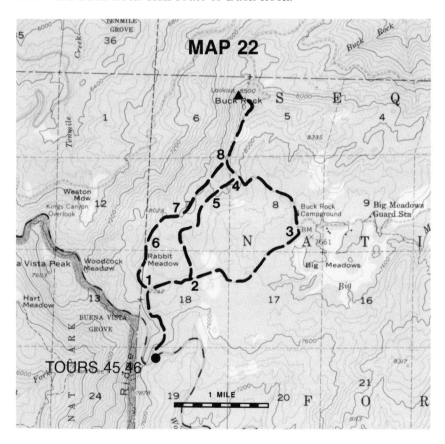

# 46 Buck Rock via Ridge

MAP 22
PAGE 105

| | |
|---|---|
| Difficulty | 3 |
| Length | 7 miles round trip |
| Elevation | 7550/+850, −850 |
| Navigation | Road and map |
| Time | Full day |
| Season | December through April |
| USGS topo | 15′ series, Giant Forest |
| Start | Big Meadows Trailhead which is located at the junction of Generals Highway (Highway 198) and the road to Big Meadows. The road to Big Meadows is on the north side of the highway and 7.0 miles southeast of the junction of Highway 180 and Generals Highway. Park either at the very start of the tour or 0.1 mile west. |

Two standard routes to Buck Rock are described in the Buck Rock tour. The route described below gets you away from those heavily used routes. Regardless of which route you choose, Buck Rock is a wonderful destination, and any two can be combined to form a loop.

From the trailhead, ski north on the snow-covered road for 0.8 mile to a road junction (1). While the other two routes to Buck Rock follow the fork to the east (right), this tour follows the fork to the northwest (left) which leads to Rabbit Meadow.

From the junction, ski 100 yards toward Rabbit Meadow to another road junction. Here, take the north (right) road and follow it for 0.3 mile to Rabbit Meadow which is on the east (right) side of the road.

Continue skiing north on the road as it parallels the meadow. When the road leaves the meadow, you should continue on it for 0.1 mile to the point where it turns south (6). Here, you must leave the road.

From the road, climb at a steep angle to the northeast for 0.3 mile to the top of Peak 8029. From the summit, descend east for 0.1 mile to a saddle (7). Continue by climbing steadily to the northeast along the ridge for 0.8 mile until you intersect a road (8). This road is part of the other routes to Buck Rock.

Ski north (left) on the road for 0.3 mile and pass to the west of a small knob. Ski another 0.4 mile on the road until you are to the east of another knob. Here, the main road turns east (right); instead you should ski northwest (left) on a lesser road to the base of Buck Rock.

*Peaceful stream*

# 47 Starlight-Big Meadows Loop

MAP 23 PAGE 109

| | |
|---|---|
| Difficulty | 3 |
| Length | 7 miles round trip |
| Elevation | 7550/ + 650, − 650 |
| Navigation | Road, marked trail and map |
| Time | Most of a day |
| Season | December through April |
| USGS topo | 15′ series, Giant Forest |
| Start | Big Meadows Trailhead which is located at the junction of Generals Highway (Highway 198) and the road to Big Meadows. The road to Big Meadows is on the north side of the highway and 7.0 miles southeast of the junction of Highway 180 and Generals Highway. Park either at the very start of the tour or 0.1 mile west. |

The usual route to Big Meadows is on a busy road. By skiing the loop described below, you can avoid this road in one direction. Since half of the tour is on the less popular Starlight Trail, you can find more of the wilderness atmosphere which one associates with ski touring.

At the starting point, ski north on the snow-covered road. After you have gone 0.2 mile, look for a marker on the east (right) side of the road which identifies the point (1) where the Starlight Trail leaves the road.

Leave the road and carefully follow the Starlight Trail markers north. Because the terrain is rolling and there are no distinct landmarks, it is very important to keep track of the markers.

From the road, ski 0.5 mile north until the trail turns east (2). In this area, you may see a trail heading north toward the road to Big Meadows. Don't follow it; instead continue southeast for 0.9 mile to the point (3) where the Snow Point Trail descends at a steep angle to the southwest.

Do not descend on the Snow Point Trail; instead continue east on the Starlight Trail along rolling terrain for 1.1 miles until you are above an arm of Big Meadows and can see the meadows to the north (4). Descend at a steep angle and ski north through the meadows to several cabins (5). One of the cabins is a warming hut operated by Wilsonia Ski Touring.

From the cabins, ski a short distance north through the trees to the road. You can follow this road west (left) back to the starting point as described in the Big Meadows tour (no. 43).

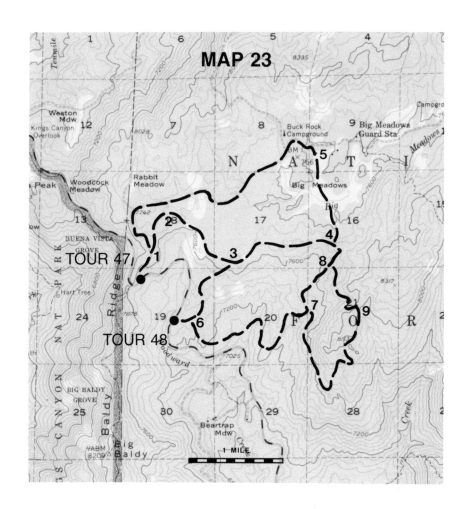

# 48 Forest-Starlight Loop

MAP 23
PAGE 109

| | |
|---|---|
| Difficulty | 3 |
| Length | 6 or 8 miles round trip |
| Elevation | 7300/ + 900, − 900 via shorter loop or 7300/ + 1050, − 1050 via longer loop |
| Navigation | Road, marked trail and map |
| Time | Most of a day |
| Season | December through April |
| USGS topo | 15′ series, Giant Forest |
| Start | Woodward Creek Trailhead, 0.3 mile south of the Montecito-Sequoia Lodge turnoff on Generals Highway (Highway 198). |

This loop gets you away from the great numbers of people who use nearby Big Meadows Trailhead. About half of this tour is on easy-to-follow roads while half is on a marked trail. You will find that the marked trail section is along excellent ski touring terrain, but you should be aware that a great deal of care is required to follow the markers.

From the trailhead, ski east on the snow-covered road for 0.1 mile to a road junction (**6**). You will return to this point via the road to the north (left).

Continue to the southeast (right) on the Forest Trail for 0.5 mile until you pass a road on your left. Ski another 1.1 miles until you pass a road on your right. Ski another 0.6 mile until you come to a road junction (**7**). At this point, you must decide whether you want to ski the 6 or 8 mile loop.

If you choose the shorter loop, take the road to the north (left). Climb for 0.8 mile to a road junction (**8**) where the short and long loops intersect again. Both routes continue northeast for 0.1 mile to a ridge.

If you choose the longer loop, at the junction (**7**) take the road to the east (right), which almost immediately turns south, for 0.1 mile until you pass a road on your right. Continue to climb gradually for 1.0 mile to the south where the road turns north.

Continue on the road, which now climbs at a steeper angle for 0.5 mile, and then climbs very gradually for 0.6 mile to a saddle (**9**). Ski down the other side of the saddle and follow the road north for 0.8 mile to a road junction (**8**) where you intersect the shorter loop. Turn northeast (right) and follow the road for 0.1 mile to a ridge.

At the ridge, leave the road and follow the Starlight Trail markers very carefully to the west for 1.2 miles over rolling terrain. Where the Snow Point Trail descends at a steep angle to the southwest, the Starlight Trail turns northwest (**3**). The exact point where the Snow Point Trail and the

110

Starlight Trail separate is not well marked, and you should refer to your map.

Descend at a steep angle on the Snow Point Trail to the southwest for 0.3 mile until you come to a road. Once on the road, follow it southwest, and you will soon pass on your right a turnoff to Montecito-Sequoia Lodge.

From the lodge turnoff, proceed south on the road for 0.5 mile to the very first road junction **(6)** you encountered on the tour. Turn west (right) and ski 0.1 mile to the trailhead.

*Getting a drink*

# 49 Sunrise-Chimney Rock Loop MAP 24
PAGE 114

| | |
|---|---|
| Difficulty | 3 |
| Length | 8 miles round trip |
| Elevation | 7300/ + 1050, − 1050 |
| Navigation | Road, marked trail and map |
| Time | Full day |
| Season | Mid-December through mid-April |
| USGS topo | 15′ series, Giant Forest |
| Start | Woodward Creek Trailhead, 0.3 mile south of the Montecito-Sequoia Lodge turnoff on Generals Highway (Highway 198). |

There are three trails in this area: the Sunrise, the Chimney Rock, and the Kaweah View. The Sunrise Trail climbs the highest and offers the best views. The tour described below combines that trail with the Chimney Rock Trail, the second highest, to form an excellent loop.

In theory you can start this tour at the point where the road to Chimney Rock leaves Generals Highway 1.0 mile southeast of Woodward Creek Trailhead. Starting at that location eliminates the one section which has poor ski touring terrain, but, unfortunately, there is no parking at that point. Therefore, short of walking the mile on the road which may not be safe or digging out a parking space, you will have to ski from Woodward Creek Trailhead.

From the parking area at the trailhead, cross to the west side of the highway, and ski south along it and adjacent to Woodward Creek. After you have gone 0.3 mile, the creek will turn away from the road. Continue to follow the creek to the southeast for 0.6 mile until you intersect a snow-covered road (1). This first 0.9 mile is in a densely wooded area and you will have to pick your own route which at times may take you away from the creek.

There is a bridge where Woodward Creek intersects the snow-covered road. If you were to follow the road northeast (left) you would reach Generals Highway in 0.3 mile. To continue on this tour, you turn south (right) and ski on the road for 0.1 mile until you reach a road junction (2). At the junction, the north (left) fork is the Kaweah View Trail and the south (straight) fork is the Chimney Rock Trail.

Continue on the Chimney Rock Trail for 0.6 mile until you reach a road junction (3) where the Chimney Rock Trail and the Sunrise Trail meet. From this junction, you can ski the loop in either direction. The counterclockwise direction is described below.

Take the fork called Sunrise Trail to the north (right) and follow it for 0.4 mile until it turns south. At this point, there are some cabins a short distance to the north of the road. Continue south on the Sunrise Trail for 0.1 mile until you reach another road junction **(4)**. Follow the southwest (left) fork for 0.9 mile to the end of the road where there is a ridge to the south which you must now climb over.

From the end of the road, follow the markers and climb for 0.1 mile to the southeast until you reach the ridge top **(5)**. The road you want to intersect is directly south of the point where you crossed the ridge. To reach the road, continue to follow the marked trail west along the south side of the ridge for 0.1 mile. The trail then turns south, and you descend for 0.2 mile to the road **(6)**.

Ski south on the road for 0.1 mile to a road junction. Head in a south-easterly direction (left) and ski downhill on the road for 1.3 miles to another road junction **(7)**. The road you intersect is the Chimney Rock Trail.

From the junction, ski north (left) on the Chimney Rock Trail for 1.3 miles until you pass a road on your left. Continue for another 100 yards to the junction **(3)** of the Sunrise Trail and the Chimney Rock Trail from where you started the loop. From here retrace your route to Woodward Creek and your car.

*Cozy cabin*

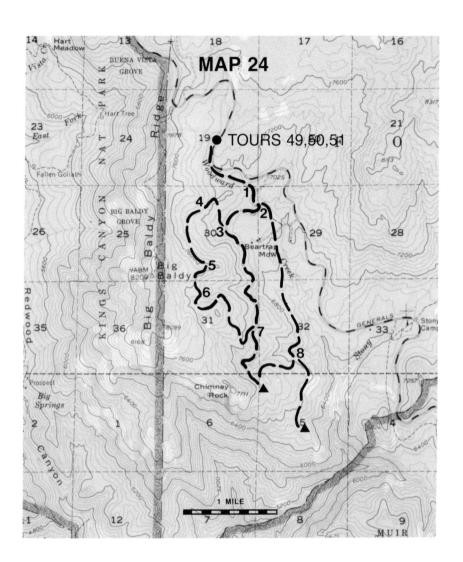

MAP 24

TOURS 49,50,51

MAP 24
PAGE 114

# Chimney Rock Trail **50**

| | |
|---|---|
| Difficulty | 3 |
| Length | Up to 8 miles round trip |
| Elevation | 7300/ + 700, − 700 |
| Navigation | Road and map |
| Time | Full day |
| Season | Mid-December through mid-April |
| USGS topo | 15′ series, Giant Forest |
| Start | Woodward Creek Trailhead, 0.3 mile south of the Montecito-Sequoia Lodge turnoff on Generals Highway (Highway 198). |

The first 0.9 mile of this tour is through dense trees. Although the skiing is not particularly good, this difficult section is guaranteed to keep the crowds away. Aside from this first section, this tour follows an almost level road to a point east of Chimney Rock. Because an ascent of Chimney Rock is very difficult and dangerous, do not expect to climb it. You should just ski as far as you like and then turn around. You can, however, connect this tour with the Kaweah View Trail tour. Directions for the connection are described in that tour.

Start this tour by following the Sunrise-Chimney Rock Loop tour (no. 49) for 1.0 mile to the junction (2) of the Chimney Rock Trail and the Kaweah View Trail. At the junction, continue on the south (straight) fork which is the Chimney Rock Trail for 0.6 mile until you reach another road junction (3) where the Chimney Rock Trail and the Sunrise Trail meet.

At this junction, the Sunrise Trail follows the road to the north (right) while you take the road to the south (straight). Ski for 100 yards until you pass a road on your right. Ski 1.3 miles farther until you come to a fork (7) in the road.

At the fork, the west (right) road is part of the Sunrise Trail and this tour continues on the east (left) road. Follow this road for 0.9 mile until you pass a road on your left. The road you pass connects the Chimney Rock Trail with the Kaweah View Trail. Continue for 100 yards to a flat area and several buildings, and you have reached the turnaround point for the Chimney Rock Trail tour.

# 51 Kaweah View Trail

MAP 24
PAGE 114

| | |
|---|---|
| Difficulty | 3 |
| Length | 10 miles round trip |
| Elevation | 7300/+750, −750 |
| Navigation | Road and map |
| Time | Full day |
| Season | Mid-December through mid-April |
| USGS topo | 15′ series, Giant Forest |
| Start | Woodward Creek Trailhead, 0.3 mile south of the Montecito-Sequoia Lodge turnoff on Generals Highway (Highway 198). |

The Kaweah View Trail leads you to a spectacular point overlooking the confluence of Stony Creek and Dorst Creek which join to form the North Fork of the Kaweah River. To the east, you also have a beautiful view of the granite face of Silliman Crest.

Start this tour by following the Sunrise-Chimney Rock Loop tour (no. 49) for 1.0 mile to the junction (2) of the Chimney Rock Trail and the Kaweah View Trail.

Continue on the Kaweah View Trail which is the north (left) fork and follow it south. Ski for 0.6 mile until you pass a road on your right, and then ski for another 0.6 mile until you pass another road on your right. Continue south for another 1.3 miles to a fork (8).

At the fork, the west (right) road connects the Kaweah View Trail with the Chimney Rock Trail. If you wish to ski to the Chimney Rock Trail, ascend the narrow and steep road for 0.5 mile until you pass a dead end road on your left. Climb for another 0.4 mile to the Chimney Rock Trail.

To continue on the Kaweah View Trail from the fork (8), ski on the east (left) fork for 1.2 miles to the obvious overlook point. You can distinguish this point by the very sharp, almost 180 degree, right turn in the road located there.

*Steep climb*

*Giant sequoia*                                                 *Kim Grandfield*

# Sequoia

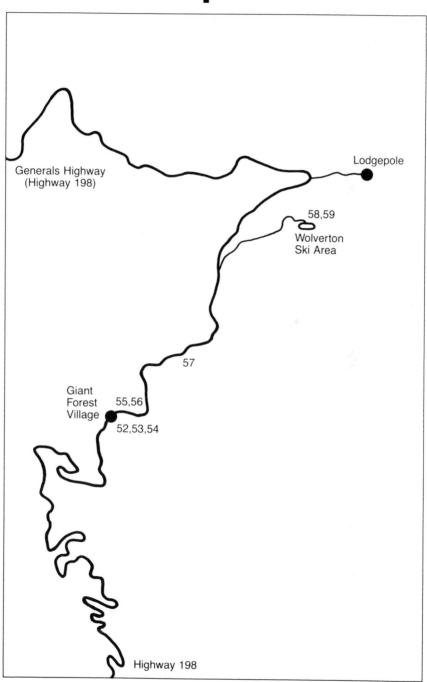

Generals Highway
(Highway 198)

Lodgepole

58,59
Wolverton
Ski Area

57

Giant
Forest
Village

55,56

52,53,54

Highway 198

# 52 Moro Rock

MAP 25
PAGE 123

| | |
|---|---|
| Difficulty | 2 |
| Length | 4 miles round trip |
| Elevation | 6400/ + 400, − 400 |
| Navigation | Road |
| Time | Few hours |
| Season | December through early April |
| USGS topo | 15′ series, Giant Forest |
| Start | Giant Forest Village on Generals Highway (Highway 198). |

Once on the summit of Moro Rock, you will understand why so many people make Moro Rock their destination; there are spectacular views in every direction. To the south is the San Joaquin Valley and to the north is Silliman Crest. Unfortunately, these views draw more than just cross-country skiers, and you should expect the trail to be pocked with the tracks of hikers. Nevertheless, this tour is an excellent one if you are just getting acquainted with ski touring.

To begin the tour, locate Crescent Meadow Road which heads south from the southwest side of the Giant Forest Village cafeteria. Walk or ski the first 0.1 mile until you pass a road on your left. Ski straight ahead on Crescent Meadow Road for 1.2 miles until you reach a road junction (1). The south (right) fork leads to Moro Rock and the north (left) fork leads to Crescent Meadow.

Stay right at the junction, and almost immediately thereafter, you will encounter a second junction. This fork is the start of the loop which leads to the base of Moro Rock; you can ski it in either direction. Halfway around the loop, you will encounter a sign indicating the base of Moro Rock.

To the base of Moro Rock, the tour is almost perfectly level. To the top of Moro Rock the route is another 0.2 mile and 300′ up. If you are going to the top, you should leave your skis at the base and hike up the steep and narrow path to the summit. The path is often very dangerous due to ice and snow, so be careful. If you do start up and conditions look poor, don't hesitate to turn around. There are fine views from various points along the way up.

MAP 25
PAGE 123

# Crescent Meadow  53

| | |
|---|---|
| Difficulty | 2 |
| Length | 5 miles round trip |
| Elevation | 6400/+ 500, − 500 |
| Navigation | Road |
| Time | Half day |
| Season | December through early April |
| USGS topo | 15' series, Giant Forest, Triple Divide Peak |
| Start | Giant Forest Village on Generals Highway (Highway 198). |

The tour to Crescent Meadow which passes among giant sequoias is an extension of the Moro Rock tour. Most tourers will find it easy to visit both places in less than a day. Like the Giant Forest Village to Moro Rock section, the terrain between Moro Rock and Crescent Meadow is gentle. In this section, however, you leave behind the tracks of hikers.

Locate Crescent Meadow Road at the southwest side of the Giant Forest Village cafeteria. You will probably be able to walk the first 0.1 mile until you pass a road on your left. Continue to ski straight ahead on Crescent Meadow Road for 1.2 miles until you encounter a road junction (**1**). The south (right) fork leads to Moro Rock. You should take the north (left) fork which leads to Crescent Meadow.

From the junction, follow the road for 0.4 mile until you come to the Tunnel Log. You can't miss this landmark because you ski right through it. Continue skiing for another 1.1 miles on the road to Crescent Meadow.

This tour ends at Crescent Meadow and returns via the same route. There are, however, two ski touring trails which continue from Crescent Meadow: the Crescent Trail and the Trail of the Sequoia. The Crescent Trail Loop tour covers the Crescent Trail, and the Sequoia Loop tour covers both the Crescent Trail and the Trail of the Sequoia.

# 54 Crescent Trail Loop

MAP 25
PAGE 123

| | |
|---|---|
| Difficulty | 3 |
| Length | 6 miles round trip |
| Elevation | 6400/ + 750, − 750 |
| Navigation | Road and marked trail |
| Time | Most of a day |
| Season | December through early April |
| USGS topo | 15′ series, Giant Forest, Triple Divide Peak |
| Start | Giant Forest Village on Generals Highway (Highway 198). |

The two loop tours through the sequoias of Giant Forest described in this guidebook are the Crescent Trail Loop and the Sequoia Loop. Both take the tourer in, out, and around the giants which make Sequoia National Park a one-of-a-kind place. The Crescent Trail Loop tour is slightly easier, although the two tours are given the same difficulty rating.

The Crescent Trail Loop tour takes you on parts of the Alta Trail, Crescent Trail, and Crescent Meadow Road. The tour is described in this direction so that the steepest section, found along the Alta Trail, is uphill, and the downhill is spread over a longer distance.

The Alta Trail leaves Giant Forest Village at its northeast end, parallels the highway on its south side, and heads toward Giant Forest Lodge. This trail is marked with yellow triangles and the image of a pine cone, but like most trail markers in Sequoia, they seem to be few and far between. Ski on the Alta Trail for 0.5 mile of easy terrain to the lodge area (2).

As you approach the lodge, locate the markers which indicate the point where the Alta Trail leaves the highway and climbs at a steep angle. Follow the markers for 1.0 mile and 600′ of elevation gain to the McKinley Tree Junction (3). In this stretch, you may need to exercise care in crossing Little Deer Creek.

When you reach the McKinley Tree Junction, take some time to enjoy the magnificent sequoias in the area. The McKinley Tree is impressive in its own right, yet nearby there are many other groups of beautiful sequoias.

At the McKinley Tree, trails are marked in five directions. Locate the yellow triangles with the image of a crescent moon. They mark the Crescent Trail and head both north and south. To the north is the General Sherman Tree and the highway; instead you should follow the markers south.

While following the Crescent Trail south, you descend gradually to Circle Meadow. Here you follow the trail which crosses to the south side of the meadow and continue for 0.2 mile to a broad saddle (4). From the saddle, descend to the south along the trail for 0.3 mile until you enter the north end of Crescent Meadow. Follow the meadow to its south end where you intersect Crescent Meadow Road **(5)**. If the conditions in the meadow are poor, ski in the trees along the west (right) side of the meadow.

To return to Giant Forest Village, follow Crescent Meadow Road west for 1.1 miles until you pass through the Tunnel Log. Proceed on the road for 0.4 mile to a road junction **(1)**. The road to the south (left) leads to Moro Rock; instead continue on the main road (straight) and ski for 1.2 miles back to Giant Forest Village.

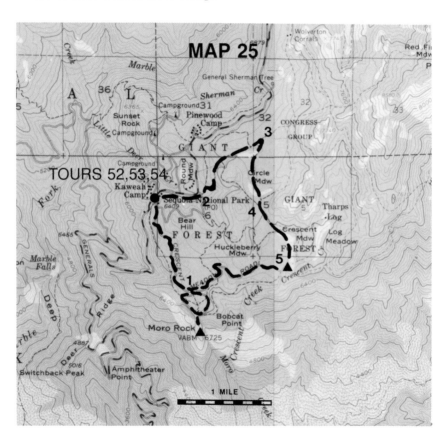

*Pear Lake*

MAP 26
PAGE 125

# Round Meadow **55**

| | |
|---|---|
| Difficulty | 1 |
| Length | Short |
| Elevation | 6400/Nil |
| Navigation | Adjacent to plowed road |
| Time | Short |
| Season | December through early April |
| USGS topo | 15' series, Giant Forest |
| Start | Round Meadow turnoff on the north side of Generals Highway (Highway 198) between Giant Forest Village and Giant Forest Lodge. |

Although Round Meadow is very small, it is the only location in the area where first-time skiers can get their balance and practice some basic techniques. When you get bored with the meadow, consider a tour to Sunset Rock or Moro Rock.

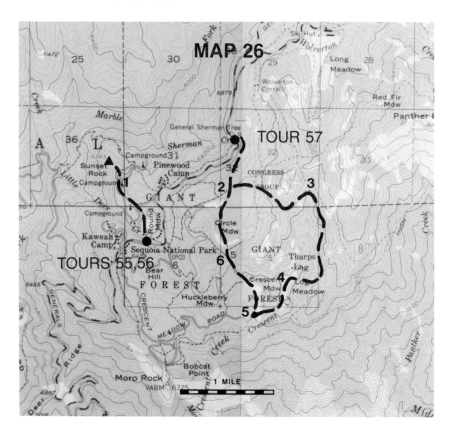

# 56 Sunset Rock

MAP 26
PAGE 125

| | |
|---|---|
| Difficulty | 2 |
| Length | 2 miles round trip |
| Elevation | 6400/ + 250, − 250 |
| Navigation | Road and marked trail |
| Time | Few hours |
| Season | December through early April |
| USGS topo | 15′ series, Giant Forest |
| Start | Round Meadow turnoff on the north side of Generals Highway (Highway 198) between Giant Forest Village and Giant Forest Lodge. |

As you might guess from the name of the tour, this tour is great to do late in the day. Sunset Rock is a large, flat, open area with fine views to the west. If you plan to wait for the sunset, be sure to bring warm clothing and a flashlight.

The route to Sunset Rock is marked with yellow triangles and the letter S. It is entirely on an unplowed road except for the last 0.2 mile.

From Round Meadow, ski north on the road which borders the west side of the meadow for 0.4 mile until you reach a high point. Here you will find roads heading to the right, left and straight ahead. You should continue straight ahead.

Continue as the road drops very slightly for 0.2 mile until you pass a road on your left. Ski for another 0.1 mile until you enter a large, flat area (1). Here, locate the markers and follow them north through the flat area. Continue to follow the markers as the trail drops for 0.2 mile to Sunset Rock.

MAP 26
PAGE 125

**Sequoia Loop** **57**

| | |
|---|---|
| Difficulty | 3 |
| Length | 6 miles round trip |
| Elevation | 6800/ + 900, − 900 |
| Navigation | Marked trail |
| Time | Most of a day |
| Season | December through early April |
| USGS topo | 15′ series, Giant Forest, Triple Divide Peak |
| Start | General Sherman Tree parking area on Generals Highway (Highway 198) 1.9 miles northeast of Giant Forest Village. |

If your one goal in visiting Sequoia National Park is to ski among the giant trees which make the park so famous, this tour should be your number one choice. This tour is extremely challenging; as it winds its way through the dense forest, it will test your ability to climb, turn, and descend in wooded terrain.

You begin this tour from the highway by skiing or walking, depending on conditions, the 0.1 mile to the General Sherman Tree, the largest living thing on earth. At this point, locate the yellow triangles with the image of a crescent moon which mark the Crescent Trail.

Ski along the trail which winds south for 0.6 mile to the McKinley Tree Junction (2). At the junction, there are five marked trails. The loop begins here and combines the Trail of the Sequoia and the Crescent Trail which meet again at Crescent Meadow. The loop may be slightly easier if you ski the Trail of the Sequoia in the southern direction.

Locate the yellow triangles with the image of a tree which mark the Trail of the Sequoia heading in an easterly direction. Ski along this trail for 0.7 mile as it climbs at first gradually, then at a steep angle until you reach a high point. In this short distance, you will pass among some of the largest sequoias in the park, including some majestic groups.

From the high point, ski northeast and descend at a steep angle for 0.3 mile to Crescent Creek (3). After you cross the creek, the trail turns south; even though the steepness of the slope lessens, the skiing is still difficult due to the dense trees. From the creek, ski for 1.0 mile until the trail turns west (right) and enters Log Meadow (4). Ski south through the meadow and turn west (right) at the end. Continue to ski for 0.1 mile until you reach Crescent Meadow (5).

The route back to the McKinley Tree Junction is via the Crescent Trail which is again marked with yellow triangles and the image of a crescent moon. Ski to the north end of Crescent Meadow. Here, enter the trees and follow the markers to the north for 0.3 mile to a broad saddle (6).

# 57

From the saddle, continue on the trail which drops to the north for 0.2 mile to Circle Meadow. Cross to the north side of the meadow and climb gradually for 0.6 mile to the McKinley Tree Junction (2).

Finally, you return to the starting point by retracing your tracks north along the Crescent Trail.

*Watch Tower*

MAP 27
PAGE 130

# Panther Gap Loop **58**

| | |
|---|---|
| Difficulty | 4 |
| Length | 6 miles round trip |
| Elevation | 7200/ + 1400, − 1400 |
| Navigation | Marked trail and map |
| Time | Full day |
| Season | December through mid-April |
| USGS topo | 15′ series, Triple Divide Peak |
| Start | Lakes Trail Trailhead located on the northern side of the Wolverton Ski Area parking area. The turnoff to the ski area is 2.8 miles northeast of Giant Forest Village on Generals Highway (Highway 198). |

If you want solitude and outstanding scenery, the tour to Panther Gap is for you. With views of the jagged, snowcapped peaks of the Great Western Divide and the San Joaquin Valley, the gap is the perfect location to enjoy a leisurely lunch.

Reaching this spectacular viewpoint, however, requires both sweat and skill. To ascend to Panther Gap, you can expect to climb the entire distance; to return to the starting point, you will face a challenging downhill run through the trees.

The first section of this tour is marked with yellow triangles and is part of the ski trail to Pear Lake. Ski northeast from the trailhead for 100 yards to the Lakes Trail and continue east up a moderate ridge for 1.0 mile. At this point, turn southeast, traverse, and climb a steep slope for 0.3 mile while following the trail.

Here (1), the trail to Pear Lake turns northeast (left) and climbs up a very steep open slope. To reach Panther Gap, continue southeast (straight) and traverse uphill. This trail is marked with yellow triangles and the image of a panther.

From the Pear Lake turnoff, ski for 0.2 mile until you cross a creek drainage which feeds Wolverton Creek. Continue for 0.1 mile more and cross Wolverton Creek itself. As the trail becomes less steep, you pass through Britten Meadow (2). From Britten Meadow, continue to climb at a steep angle to the south for 0.4 mile to Panther Gap (3).

Panther Gap is the obvious saddle between Panther Peak and Peak 9975; to its south the slope drops away at a very steep angle. If after a storm the trees at the gap are encrusted with ice, be careful where you sit.

To complete the loop, leave Panther Gap by entering the trees to the west. Again, the markers are yellow triangles with the image of a panther. You follow the trail which traverses to the west and slightly north, remains level, and is below the summer trail. From the gap, ski for 0.5 mile until you reach Panther Meadow (**4**).

From Panther Meadow, continue on the trail to the northwest for 0.4 mile until you round a spur. Head southwest for 0.2 mile more and pass Red Fir Meadow (**5**) which is below the trail.

From Red Fir Meadow, ski in a westerly direction for 0.3 mile until the trail turns to the southwest. Continue for 0.2 mile and enter a clearing (**6**) from which you can look downhill at Long Meadow. At this point, do not attempt to descend directly to the meadow and the ski area below. Even though some old trail markers lead you in this direction, it is a poor choice due to the high probability of ice and avalanche conditions.

Instead, traverse and descend to the southwest for 0.2 mile. When the slopes become less steep, turn west and ski for 0.3 mile to the junction of the Alta Trail and the Panther Trail (**7**); this junction is located at a gap above the canyon which drains toward the ski area.

From the junction, ski north along a ridge and follow the Alta Trail markers which are yellow triangles with the image of a pine cone for 0.5 mile until you reach a high point. Just north of this point, find the top of one of the chairlifts which descends to the ski area. From here, pick the best route down to the lodge.

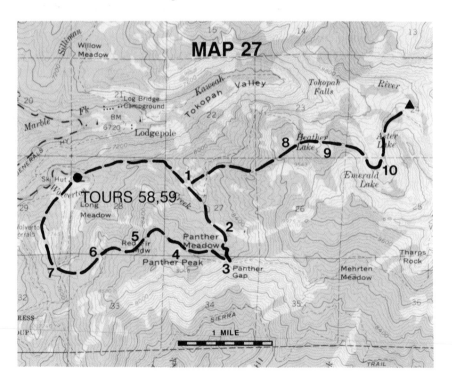

*Pear Lake Hut*

# **59** Pear Lake

MAP 27
PAGE 130

| | |
|---|---|
| Difficulty | 4 |
| Length | 9 miles round trip |
| Elevation | 7200/ + 2600, − 2600 |
| Navigation | Marked trail and map |
| Time | One very long day or two days round trip |
| Season | December through mid-April |
| USGS topo | 15′ series, Triple Divide Peak |
| Start | Lakes Trail Trailhead located on the northern side of the Wolverton Ski Area parking area. The turnoff to the ski area is 2.8 miles northeast of Giant Forest Village on Generals Highway (Highway 198). |

The tour to Pear Lake Hut provides an excellent opportunity to visit the High Sierra in its winter splendor. Built forty years ago from native stone and lodgepole pine logs, this rustic shelter is a ranger station in the summer months. Converted to a ski hut in the winter, it is a haven from which to explore the Sequoia backcountry around Pear Lake, Alta Peak and the Tablelands.

The hut, which sleeps ten, is open to the public by reservation only. The Sequoia Natural History Association operates the hut, for which they collect a fee, and supplies fuel for the heater, cooking stove and lanterns. Reservations should be made well in advance by contacting:

> Chief Ranger's Office
> Ash Mountain Headquarters
> Sequoia and Kings Canyon National Parks
> Three Rivers, California 93271

The 4.6 mile tour to Pear Lake Hut is very challenging and also very rewarding. The most difficult section is the 2000′ which must be ascended in the first half of the tour and descended on the return. The route is marked with yellow triangles, but you must use considerable care in following them, since there are few markers in some areas.

Although it is not difficult for advanced skiers to make a one-day, round trip tour to the Pear Lake area, the ski touring opportunities and the beauty of the area are so great that it is a shame to miss exploring the Pear Lake area. Once at Pear Lake Hut, the possibilities for day tours are numerous. Plan at least one layover day in order to enjoy the region.

From the trailhead, ski northeast for 100 yards to the Lakes Trail and continue east up a moderate ridge. Follow the ridge for 1.0 mile until the trail turns southeast. Continue on the trail as it traverses and climbs a steep slope for 0.3 mile until the Pear Lake Trail turns northeast (left) **(1)**.

It is very important that you look closely for this turnoff. If you miss it, you will end up on the Panther Trail toward Panther Gap.

At the Pear Lake Trail turnoff, look for a very steep, open slope. Climb the slope, switchbacking where necessary, and head northeast. When the route enters the woods again, you continue to climb at a steep angle to the east. Eventually, the route starts to climb more moderately, and Heather Gap (8) is just ahead. The distance from the Panther Trail to Heather Gap is 1.4 miles.

Not far to the north of Heather Gap is the Watch Tower, a 1000' cliff which drops to Tokopah Falls and the Marble Fork of the Kaweah River. Neither the top of the cliff nor the drainage below is a safe place for skiers. You can get good views of the Watch Tower from many points near Pear Lake.

Heather Gap is aptly referred to as "the hump" because after climbing up one side, the route drops down the other. Ski east for 0.3 mile to Heather Lake (9) which is 200' below. From the lake, climb east to a bench, and then traverse east and south toward Emerald Lake. Finally, you should lose some altitude and drop into the Emerald Lake outlet drainage (10). The distance from Heather Lake to the Emerald Lake outlet drainage is 0.8 mile.

Cross the drainage, climb at a fairly steep angle to the north, and round the corner of a ridge. If you have climbed enough, you will find a short downhill run to the northeast and to the ski hut. Pear Lake Hut is located 0.4 mile north of Pear Lake along Pear Lake Creek and 0.2 mile above the junction of the creek with the Marble Fork of the Kaweah River.

Unfortunately, much of the terrain in the Pear Lake area is perfect for avalanches. Be sure to exercise caution while touring in the area.

*Marble Fork of the Kaweah River*

# Nordic Ski Centers

The nordic centers listed here provide ski touring services and facilities, and are a good source for current snow, weather and avalanche conditions.

### YOSEMITE MOUNTAINEERING SCHOOL

| | |
|---|---|
| Location | Yosemite Valley in Yosemite National Park. |
| Address | Yosemite National Park, CA 95389 |
| Phone | 209-372-1244 |
| Elevation | 6200' at Crane Flat and 7200' at Badger Pass |

### GRANT GROVE SKI TOURING

| | |
|---|---|
| Location | Grant Grove in Kings Canyon National Park. |
| Address | Kings Canyon National Park, CA 93633 |
| Phone | 209-335-2314 |
| Elevation | 6400' to 7600' |

### WILSONIA SKI TOURING

| | |
|---|---|
| Location | Wilsonia Lodge in Kings Canyon National Park. |
| Address | P.O. Box 855, Kings Canyon National Park, CA 93633 |
| Phone | 209-335-2404 |
| Elevation | 6400' to 7600' |

### MONTECITO-SEQUOIA CROSS COUNTRY SKI CENTER

| | |
|---|---|
| Location | Between Kings Canyon and Sequoia National Parks on Generals Highway, 9 miles south of Grant Grove. |
| Address | 1485 Redwood Drive, Los Altos, CA 94022 |
| Phone | 415-967-8612 (reservations) or 209-565-3388 (lodge) |
| Elevation | 7500' |

### SEQUOIA SKI TOURING

| | |
|---|---|
| Location | Giant Forest in Sequoia National Park. |
| Address | Sequoia National Park, CA 93262 |
| Phone | 209-565-3461 |
| Elevation | 6400' to 7200' |